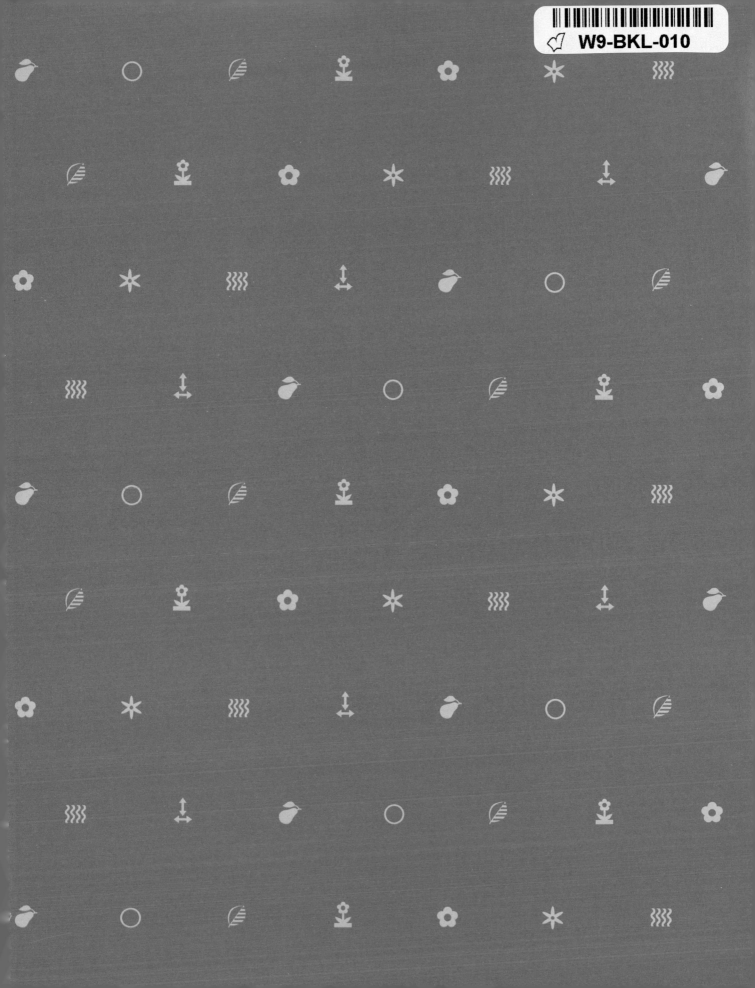

Plants for Family Gardens

CASSELL'S DIRECTORY OF

Plants for Family Gardens

EVERYTHING YOU NEED TO CREATE A GARDEN

LUCY HUNTINGTON

CASSELL&CO

Distributed in the United States of America
by Sterling Publishing Co., Inc.
387 Park Avenue South, New York, NY 10016-8810

A CIP Catalogue record for this book is
available from the British Library

ISBN 0 304 35604 2

This book was conceived, designed, and produced by
THE IVY PRESS LIMITED
The Old Candlemakers, West Street,
Lewes, East Sussex BN7 2NZ

Creative Director: PETER BRIDGEWATER
Designers: AXIS DESIGN
Editorial Director: DENNY HEMMING
Managing Editor: ANNE TOWNLEY
Illustrations: VANESSA LUFF & PETER BULL
Picture Researcher: LIZ EDDISON

Originated and printed by Hong Kong Graphic, Hong Kong

This book is typeset in Linotype Perpetua and Univers

CASSELL & CO
Wellington House, 125 Strand, London WC2R 0BB

ACKNOWLEDGMENTS

t *top* **b** *below* **l** *left* **r** *right*   ***Directory a–f***, *starting from top*

Liz Eddison 6, 7, 18t,b, 21, 26, 34r, 36l, 37r, 38r, 42r, 64d, 102c / Natural & Oriental Water Gardens 40r / Designer: Georgina Steeds 23, 30
The Garden Picture Library Geoff Dann 77b / Sunniva Harte 75c, 79b / J.S Sira 44 / Juliette Wade 22b, 36r
John Glover 2,4,5, 10-11,12t,b, 14t,b, 15, 16t,b, 20t,b, 22t, 24, 32–33, 34l, 35l,r, 37l, 39l,r 40, 41l,r, 42l, 43r, 48, 50, 51, 55, 57, 58, 60–61 / Designer: Terry Hill, Hampton Court 99 1 / Designer: Barbara Hunt 38l / Designer: Alan Titchmarsh 13, 17, 19
Lucy Huntington 28
Peter McHoy 64a,b,c,f, 65a,c,d,e, 66a,b,c,d,e,f, 67a,b,c,d,f, 68a,b,c,e,f, 69c,e,f, 70a–f, 71a,b,d,e,f, 72a–f, 73a,b,c,d,e, 74a,c,d,e,f, 75a,d,e,f, 76b,d, 77c,e, 78b,d,e,f, 79c,d,e, 80c,e, 81b,c,d, 82b,c, 83b,c,e,f, 84a,c,d,e,f, 85a–f, 86a,b,d,e,f, 87a–f, 88a,b,d,e,f, 89c,f, 90a,c,d,e,f, 91a,c,f, 92b,c,d,e, 93a–f, 94b,c,d,e,f, 95a,b,e,f, 96a,c,e,f, 97b,c,d,f, 98a,c,e,f, 99a,b,c,d,e, 100a–f, 101a–f, 102b,d,e,f, 103c,d,e,f, 104a,c,d,e, 105a,b,e,f, 106b,d,e, 107a,e,f
The Harry Smith Collection 64e, 65b, 67e, 68d, 69a,b,d, 71c, 73f, 74b, 75b, 76a,d, 77a,d,f, 78a,c, 79a,f, 80a,b,d,f, 81e,f, 82d,e,f, 83a,d, 86c, 88c, 89a,b,d,e, 91b,d,e, 92a,f, 94a, 95c,d, 96b,d, 97a, 98b,d, 99f, 102a, 103a,b, 104b,f, 105c,d, 106c,f, 107b,c,d
David Squire 65f, 76c,f, 81a, 82a, 84b, 90b, 97e, 106a

CONTENTS

INTRODUCTION

Families need gardens: they need an outside space in which to relax, play, dream dreams and grow plants. Most of us have a garden, however microscopic, and many of us have families, but rarely are the two things considered together. Gardens tend to be seen as places in which knowledgeable experts grow specialist plants, not as places where everybody — whatever their age, skills, and interests — can have fun exploring and learning to grow a whole range of wonderful plants.

Gardening is not difficult but is a skill readily acquired by anyone, whatever their age and background, and once acquired it can lead to a lifetime of pleasure. Nor does looking after the garden have to be a chore: the key is to keep the garden simple and to discover which plants the various family members enjoy looking after. If nobody likes roses, then exclude them from the garden; if someone enjoys growing vegetables, then have a vegetable garden; if a teenager turns out to be an alpine enthusiast, then give him or her a rock garden. Small children should be encouraged to sow seeds even if they insist on digging them up every day to see how they have grown! There are no right or wrong types of garden or plants, only the wrong choices made by gardeners.

This book is about both planning and planting your family garden: at its core is a directory of the best plants for growing in a family garden, and it also contains lots of exciting ideas for using the featured plants to create an

outside space which is interesting and fun for everyone. Large gardens offer the opportunity to give a separate area to each member of the family, but they can be hard work because they need a lot of maintenance. Small gardens are easier to look after, but need more careful planning to make good use of the space.

The book is divided into three parts. The first explains how to plan your family garden. It starts by showing you how to decide on the most appropriate garden, which will depend on the number of family members, their ages, their particular interests, and the space available. It shows you how to work out what each member of the family wants to be included in the garden and then how to create a garden which is just right for your family—and even how to make sure the family pets can enjoy the garden.

The second part of the book will help you to make informed decisions in selecting materials, features, and plants for your garden. There is practical advice on choosing and growing plants, and there are details of water features and play equipment.

LEFT *A built-in barbecue on the terrace with an attractive herb garden close by offers a pretty setting for family occasions and for entertaining friends in the open air.*

PLANT DIRECTORY

The final section of this book is the plant directory, which gives details of the most popular and attractive plants for growing in a family garden. Emphasis is placed on tough plants which are easy to grow, as the plants may have to cope with being trampled by dogs, nibbled by pet rabbits, or being thumped by the odd football. There may also be limited time available for gardening and the adults concerned may be very new to the task, so the plants need to be capable of thriving even if totally neglected. But even the toughest plants can be beautiful and there are plenty of colorful flowers to ensure your garden looks attractive throughout the year.

Safety is a major consideration where there are small children involved. With this in mind, we have devoted part of the plant directory to plants you may wish to exclude

ABOVE A family garden needs to have enough variety and interest to please all the generations that use it.

from your garden, including plants which cause skin allergies, poisonous plants, and plants with prickles and thorns. It is important that these plants can be easily recognized and then removed, if necessary.

AN OUTSIDE ROOM

Planning this outside room has not been given enough attention by garden writers. You can seldom find the information you particularly need to help you to understand and guide the gardening interests of each member of the family. This book encourages families to get outside and use their garden.

Family gardens should be safe, secure havens in which every member of the family, whatever their age, can grow plants and enjoy gardening as well as relax, play, explore and entertain. In this book you will find all you need to ensure that the possibility becomes a reality.

HOW TO USE THIS BOOK

*C*assell's *Garden Directories have been conceived and written to appeal both to gardening beginners and to confident gardeners who need advice for a specific project. Each book focuses on a particular type of garden, drawing on the experience of an established expert. The emphasis is on a practical and down-to-earth approach that takes account of the space, time, and money that you have available. The ideas and techniques in these books will help you to produce an attractive and manageable garden that you will enjoy for years to come.*

Cassell's Directory of Plants for Family Gardens looks at ways to make use of garden space to create an outside room that offers something to all the members of your family. The book is divided into three sections. The opening section, *Planning Your Garden*, considers the requirements of different age groups and looks at some of the issues you will need to address. There are also three inspirational garden plans for making the most of a surburban garden, a small country garden, and a very small town or city garden.

Part Two of the book, *Creating Your Garden*, moves on to the nitty-gritty of putting your ideas into practice. This section opens with some advice on the range of different features that you can choose from, such as furniture, hard surfaces, play equipment, and fountains and ponds. There is also advice on producing a lawn that will be appropriate for the range of demands that your family is going to put on it; also on the selection, buying, and planting of appropriate shrubs, herbs, and flowers.

The remainder of Part Two is packed with practical information on basic techniques such as sowing and feeding plants, repairing damaged lawns, making compost, and supporting climbers. This section then encourages you to put your skills to work with a series of specific projects, such as making wildlife areas and creating a children's garden. There are step-by-step illustrations throughout this section that show clearly and simply what you need to do to achieve the best results. Also included are handy hints and tips, points to watch out for, and star plants that are particularly suitable for the projects that are described.

The final part of the book, *The Plant Directory*, is a comprehensive listing of all the plants mentioned in the earlier sections, together with other plants that are suitable for a family garden. Each plant is illustrated, and symbols add information on appropriate growing conditions, speed of growth, and ease of maintenance. The season of interest for each plant is also given.

GARDEN DESIGNS are included to inspire you to great things in your own garden.

COLOR PHOTOGRAPHS show what can be achieved with a little effort and imagination.

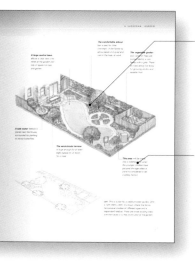

3D PLANS show the best planting plan for you to achieve the ideal outcome

THE KEY FEATURES of the plan are detailed to help you visualize the final effect.

CHOICES show a selection of plants, garden furniture, or other features that might be appropriate in your garden.

COLOR PHOTOGRAPHS help you to decide on the appropriate feature for your garden.

EXPLANATORY TEXT describes the various possibilities available in each category.

THE CHECKLIST details important things to look out for in choosing garden features.

CLEAR ILLUSTRATIONS show each step of the process.

PRACTICAL SUGGESTIONS give useful information on basic techniques and garden projects.

WATCHPOINTS BOXES give a checklist of cautions and problems to look out for.

THE PLANT DIRECTORY is organized into categories, making it simple to find a particular type of plant.

CLEAR DESCRIPTIVE TEXT details the appearance and the appropriate growing conditions for each plant.

COLOR PHOTOGRAPHS clearly identify each plant listed.

THE SYMBOLS PANEL gives important information on features such as speed of growth and shade-tolerance.

SIDEBAR shows at a glance the seasons of interest for each plant.

9

PLANNING YOUR GARDEN

1

Before starting to design your ideal family garden, you need to consider the various requirements of all the family members, including the pets. Finding space for a terrace for family meals, a barbecue, a sandbox and paddling pool, a treehouse and climbing frame, some areas for privacy and peace, not to mention beds and borders for the gardening members of the family may sound like a tall order. However, with careful planning you should be able to satisfy at least some of each person's wishes.

LEFT *Even a tiny garden can have a patch of lawn for children to run, jump, and play on.*

WHAT IS A FAMILY GARDEN?

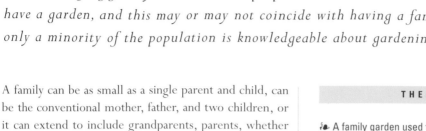

A family garden is any outside space that is expected to fulfill the needs of a range of family members. Most people at some time in their lives will have a garden, and this may or may not coincide with having a family, but only a minority of the population is knowledgeable about gardening.

A family can be as small as a single parent and child, can be the conventional mother, father, and two children, or it can extend to include grandparents, parents, whether biological or otherwise, and any number of children, step-children, aunts, uncles, and partners. In this book, a family has been taken to mean all the people, related or not, who share the same outside space, and will usually include one or more children.

Families also include all ages, from the new baby to toddlers, school children, teenagers, young adults, and right through to middle-aged and elderly relatives. The needs of an 80-year-old great granny are going to be very different to those of a newborn baby, a rebellious teenager, or young parents. Family gardens are often taken to imply families with children, but in this book we have tried to look at the needs of all age groups.

LEFT *This narrow garden has been built on three levels to make good use of the limited space. Parents can relax on the terrace while the children play on the lawn below.*

THEN AND NOW

🐚 A family garden used to be a place in which vegetables were grown to feed the family; there was plenty of space to hang out the washing; and there was a patch of lawn on which the baby's stroller was put out in the afternoon. Now the family garden can be any garden, whatever its size and location, in which all the various members of the family can indulge in gardening or any other outdoor activity.

CHILDREN OF ALL AGES

Babies are easy to accommodate in the garden as they just need a flat, smooth surface in the shade on which they can lie and play. Once they can crawl and start walking, however, the garden becomes an exciting place to explore. At this stage, safety becomes a major consideration, and plenty of playing space should be provided within sight of the house. More details and ideas for small children in the garden are on pages 18 and 19.

Gardens are great places for school-age children, especially if they can have their own space where they can dig, play, and even garden without annoying other members of the family—see pages 20 and 21 for further ideas.

If your family includes teenagers, then you already know that, if they use the garden, it is for talking to friends, playing music, sleeping, and eating. They value their privacy and want their own private space. In a larger garden it may be possible to offer them their own area at the far end. Ideally this should be screened and include an area for sitting and lounging or, if possible, a couple of trees with a hammock and even a large swing. Add a locked shed in which they can keep their special bits and pieces, and they should be happy.

PARENTS NEED GARDENS

Parents are often forgotten when planning gardens. Every effort is made to accommodate sandboxes, swings, and play houses for the children, and the fact that there are adult members of the family can appear unimportant. However, once issues of safety are resolved, then there should be room for comfortable chairs on the terrace for relaxing and the inclusion of the borders and garden features that the adults will enjoy.

KEEPING GRANDPARENTS HAPPY

Today an extended family may well include a grandparent, who may or may not be elderly, and there may be visiting members of the family who are less active than they used to be. The family garden needs to cater for their needs, which may include somewhere to sit out in the sun or the shade, interesting things to look at, and perhaps their own area of garden. People who have retired from

work are often avid gardeners, in which case the plants and garden features that are chosen will need to be those that they enjoy looking after.

FAMILY PETS

These all-important four-legged family members should not be forgotten in planning your garden: see pages 22 and 23 for details of how to cater for their various needs and requirements.

LEFT *The end of this garden has been laid out with a summer-house and a sandbox.*

WHAT DO YOU NEED IN YOUR FAMILY GARDEN?

Most gardens are modest in size, and it is almost inevitable that the limited room available will necessitate some careful planning. It is always worth preparing a checklist of activities, features, and plants that you want to include. You will, of course, have to prioritize your needs and desires, working together as a family to decide on joint goals. Try to see the limits imposed on you by your garden— whether of size, shape, or location—not as problems but as challenges.

When only one member of the family has charge of the garden and dictates how it is to be planted and developed, then there is only one person whose wishes need to be satisfied. For a whole family, however, there probably needs to be a more democratic process at work. Even when members of the family are too young to put their gardening preferences into words, their particular requirements should also be taken into account *(see pages 18 and 19)*.

There are various different ways of looking at how you might plan the garden, and you might start by considering the type of garden that you all want. It might include some or all of the following features, depending on the resources at your disposal:

BELOW *A bird feeder is a perennial favorite in the family garden.*

HINTS AND TIPS
✿ Do consult all members of the family in the planning process.
✿ Do plan carefully.
✿ Do consider safety first.
✿ Do look at how long an interest is likely to last.
✿ Do keep it simple where possible.
✿ Don't sacrifice your garden to the children.
✿ Don't forget the family pets.
✿ Don't forget maintenance.

❖ An outdoor living space for eating, reading, and relaxing.
❖ A place for entertaining friends and family and for holding parties.
❖ An adventure playground for children, with slides, swings, rope ladders, treehouses, and a jungle gym.
❖ A gardener's garden full of roses, herbaceous borders, trees, hedges, spring bulbs, and shrubs for autumn color.
❖ A productive garden full of vegetables and fruit.
❖ A wildlife garden with birds, bees, and butterflies.
❖ A tranquil oasis of peace, quiet, and gentle fountains.
❖ A place for recreation and exercise—complete with a ball field, swimming pool, and tennis court.
❖ A pets' corner for dogs, cats, rabbits, and guinea pigs.

MAKING LISTS

One way of sorting out what is wanted is to sit everyone down and ask them to make a list of what they would like in a garden. Babies' considerations will have to be taken

MOTHER AND FATHER
- [ ] Terrace for family meals
- [ ] Barbecue
- [ ] Safety
- [ ] Water
- [ ] Time to enjoy
- [ ] Somewhere to read
- [ ] Rose arch/beds
- [ ] Scent
- [ ] Camellias
- [ ] Easy maintenance

GRANDPARENTS
- [ ] Comfortable chair
- [ ] Roses
- [ ] Herb garden
- [ ] Place to watch grandchildren playing
- [ ] Bird bath
- [ ] Water feature

16-YEAR-OLD GIRL
- [ ] My own space
- [ ] Hammock
- [ ] Swimming pool
- [ ] No kids
- [ ] No gardening
- [ ] Music

5-YEAR-OLD GIRL
- [ ] Pink flowers
- [ ] Pretty flowers
- [ ] My own garden
- [ ] Playhouse
- [ ] Swing
- [ ] Picnic place

UNCLE
- [ ] Vegetable garden
- [ ] Shed
- [ ] Greenhouse
- [ ] Peace and quiet
- [ ] Barbecue

10-YEAR-OLD BOY
- [ ] Frogs and insects
- [ ] Adventure playground
- [ ] Campsite
- [ ] Barbecue
- [ ] A private den
- [ ] Ball field

3-YEAR-OLD BOY
- [ ] Paddling pool
- [ ] Sandbox
- [ ] Tadpoles
- [ ] Slide and swings
- [ ] Fish

into account by the adults, but allow children who are old enough to contribute their own ideas. It may help in the list-making if memory joggers are used, for instance suggesting that everybody puts down their favorite flowers. It is useful if family members prioritize their chosen features, stating which are the most important.

ABOVE A special corner brought to life with a child's "trough garden" filled with nasturtiums and French marigolds.

An alternative is for one member of the family to make a list of everything that could be included in a garden and then to circulate the list for each family member to check the items of importance to them.

Lists can include features (a paddling pool, a wildlife pond); feelings (peace, relaxation, excitement); use of space (place to entertain friends, to read, to have adventures); or types of plants (roses, pink flowers, scented, apple trees).

MAKING CHOICES

When the lists are complete, you can see if any of the items on different lists are compatible and which wishes are totally impossible. Looking at the sample lists above, several family members want a barbecue, so that needs to be considered; a swimming pool is probably just a dream given the cost, space, and safety aspects, but the football player might be satisfied with goalposts if he cannot have a whole ball field. Everybody wants their own space, so plan for some secluded sitting areas, and a rose garden with a rose arch would keep several people happy. Space needs to be found for a sandbox and a paddling pool, if possible, and somewhere for frogs. By considering everybody's wishes, a compromise can be reached.

AN OUTSIDE ROOM

*T*he garden should be seen as another room in which all the activities that take place inside the house—eating, sleeping, relaxing, playing, entertaining, and even cooking—can occur. A paved terrace adjacent to the house usually provides the space for this outside room.

Measure how much room is taken up if all the family members sit together around a table, remembering that you need space to push a chair away from the table to get up. A lawn adjacent to the terrace allows family and guests to spread out into the garden, but when the lawn is wet everybody will want to stay on the terrace. A paved area of 12 x 15ft (3.6 x 4.5m) allows eight people to sit comfortably around a table; extend this to 13 x 18ft (4 x 5.4m) and there is room to stand for drinks beforehand.

POSITION OF THE TERRACE

If you want breakfast in the sun, the terrace needs to be on the east side of the house; for a sunny lunch, place the terrace to the south; and for the warmth of the setting sun for an evening meal or barbecue, then a west-facing terrace is perfect. A terrace facing southwest is ideal, allowing some shade if the sun is too hot and providing a warm spot for afternoon siestas and evening parties.

When orienting the terrace, take account of the position of any outside doors or French windows that give easy access to the house. If the only access is a door around the corner from the terrace, plan a wide path between them.

EATING IN THE GARDEN

Most families will want to eat, at least occasionally, in the garden, and some may even want to dine out every time the weather is remotely warm and dry enough. Main meals

ABOVE *A very stylish modern terrace with wooden decking to match the indoor flooring.*

are best served at a table on the terrace, which will be close to the house for serving and clearing up. Other meals may be more fun as picnics carried into the garden.

Barbecues can be built into the terrace, or they can be freestanding, sometimes with wheels so that they can be moved away after use. They range in size from small to giant, but if you are new to barbecue cookery, get a small portable one first so that you can find the best spot for it—out of the wind, near the kitchen, and accessible to both cooks and guests—and also to see if you enjoy barbecuing. If you decide to proceed, buy a larger and more robust portable barbecue, or, if you are really enthusiastic, build your own.

POINTS TO CONSIDER

🔸 Decisions on a barbecue should be made by the whole family, as noncooking members are often quite happy to take over the job of barbecuing from the regular cook.

🔸 Use garden torches and candles with caution, always placing them out of any wind and where there is no danger of fire, should they fall over.

FAMILY GATHERINGS

Gardens are wonderful places for family gatherings and parties, allowing for a convivial atmosphere and offering plenty of room for mingling, while providing secluded corners for more intimate moments. You can create extra seating by including some raised beds or low walls to the side of the terrace; the walls should have wide copings at sitting height (18in/45cm for adults and 12–16in/ 30–40cm for children) on which you can place cushions when seats are needed. Raised beds allow plants to be placed safely out of the way of children playing on the terrace, and low walls give a greater feeling of privacy.

For children's birthday parties the garden is an ideal setting, providing the weather is dry and not too windy. Any mess can be easily cleared up and there is plenty of room for organized games to get rid of youthful energy. Tea and coffee can be served around the table or perhaps as a special picnic, always a popular treat.

LIGHTING

If you do lots of entertaining, or the family likes to use the garden in the evening, then you might consider lighting the terrace or perhaps the whole of the garden. Candles and lamps are convenient for occasional use, but a full-scale electric lighting plan can transform an ordinary family garden into a place of magic and mystery. There are many light fittings from which to choose, but always use lights and cabling that are designed for outside use. You should obtain the advice of a qualified electrician before beginning any kind of electrical installation.

BELOW *A patio garden with dinner set for two—a welcome treat after the children have gone to bed and the buckets and tools and tricycles have been cleared away.*

UNDERFIVES IN THE GARDEN

If you have young children, your garden should be designed to provide a safe outside space for them to explore. During the first two years, a child progresses from a helpless, totally dependent being, to a speaking, running person with a mind and a will of its own. The baby safely surrounded with a few toys on a rug very quickly becomes an active toddler trying to climb trees or escape over the garden gate.

Traditionally, the garden was the place in which babies were placed to sleep in their strollers in the afternoon, protected by a net against marauding cats, and with a sunshade to screen them from direct sunlight. This established part of the daily routine ended with the demise of the large stroller in favor of more portable buggies. Now babies are more likely to sleep in the house and spend their waking hours in the garden.

Much of a baby's time can be spent in the garden, as long as there is a suitable surface and the weather is fine. A padded mat on the paving or a rug on the grass provides a comfortable base for most activities, but do remember that small babies should always be in the shade, even if the sun is not actually shining. The drawback to outside playing is that babies must not be left alone, particularly when they begin to crawl; when awake, they will demand the full attention of at least one member of the family, and will need a range of toys to keep them happily occupied.

TODDLERS AND THE UNDERTHREES

Once children can walk they are able to get everywhere, but because they are incapable of understanding the meaning of danger, safety becomes a top priority *(see pages 48 and 49)*. They need a flat part of the garden allocated to their play needs that can be used all year, preferably with some grass for use in summer and a paved area for year-round play. For their safety, the area needs to be in full view of the windows of the house at all times. There should also be a shady space for when the sun gets too hot, as small children are very susceptible to heatstroke.

The most sensible areas are the terrace and that part of the lawn nearest the house. The only problems are that the space may be taken up by garden furniture, which can create interesting but potentially dangerous obstacles for small children, and that their brightly colored toys are an

---

WATCHPOINTS

🍂 If you have very young children, take particular care on where you choose to site a pool. Children should be in view at all times, as a young infant can drown in just a few inches of water.

🍂 Make sure all boundaries are secure and childproof.

🍂 Avoid rough surfaces such as gravel for play areas.

LEFT *This blue rubberized path makes an ideal surface for toddlers and wheeled toys, although most people will probably not want to customize their garden to this extent.*

eyesore for other members of the family. The answer is to bring the toys inside after use and to have easily movable garden furniture if the terrace space is restricted.

SANDBOXES

From the earliest age children love digging and filling. You can construct a simple sandbox by digging a hole in the lawn, lining the sides of the hole with wooden boards and the base with 4in (10cm) of coarse gravel covered with a water-permeable fabric membrane, and then filling the hole with sand. An alternative is to dig a hole in the terrace, put blocks at the sides to support the paving, and line and fill as before. The third option, and usually the most popular, is to buy a preformed plastic sandbox that can sit on the lawn or terrace. The problems here are that these sandboxes are usually fairly small, and the bright color of the plastic is visually intrusive. Choose a sandbox that has a well-fitting lid in order to prevent cats using it and to keep the sand dry.

Paddling pools are almost synonymous with sandboxes, the two re-creating the seaside experience in the garden. A small collapsible pool is most sensible for the early years, as it can be put away easily after use.

GARDENING WITH SMALL CHILDREN

Once children are toddling, they will want to be involved with whatever is going on, especially if it looks messy, so if you try to garden they will want to garden with you. Buy a set of children's gardening tools, including a wheelbarrow, trowel, fork, rake, spade, and watering can, and allow them to work with you. It may take longer to get the work done, but everybody should have fun, and you will be preparing the ground for their green-fingered future. Watering seems to hold a fascination for this age group, so allow children to help; it may not be very effective but they will enjoy themselves.

ABOVE *A small sandbox can be tucked into a corner of the garden. Add a hose and you have the seaside at home!*

Do remember that fun activities in the garden do not necessarily involve sophisticated and expensive toys. Slides and swings are nice if you have them, but the old tried-and-tested favorites such as balls, bouncers, buckets and spades, and blocks are still the best.

TRIKES, BIKES, AND TOY CARS

All children like getting around on wheels, so you may need to accommodate tricycles, bikes, toy cars, and scooters. Their own garden is by far the safest space in which to learn to master new skills, and an area of dry, close-mown grass is ideal. As riders become more adventurous, they need a smooth, hard riding surface: asphalt or concrete is best but neither is very attractive. An area of well-laid paving within sight of the house windows is perfect for the tricycle riders, but a negotiable path around the garden is greater fun for more adventurous riders.

SCHOOL-AGE CHILDREN

Once children have reached school age, they can be given the freedom of the garden. This is an age when space is needed to kick footballs, build camps, dig holes, and perhaps have their own garden. The garden needs to be a place for adventure and exploration, with hidden secret places and wildlife corners. The only problem is keeping boisterous ten-year-olds away from other members of the family who want peace and quiet.

The answer is to separate some of the activities for this age group into their own space where physically possible. Within this area they should be free to play games, dig holes, and entertain their friends, but they must understand that other areas of the garden are to be shared and that some areas are off-limits or at least to be treated with respect. The same delineation should be made in the garden as is found in the house, with children's bedrooms and playrooms being their areas, the family sitting room being shared, and the parents' bedroom off limits. This idea works well when the garden is large enough for several separate spaces, but may be difficult to achieve in smaller gardens. Where space is restricted, family members will simply have to learn to accommodate one another's needs.

ACTIVITIES

Children in this age group vary enormously in the activities they enjoy. Some will like studying insects and plants and reading quietly; others want to do nothing but kick footballs and play rowdy games; yet others will play long games of make-believe in the undergrowth. Wait until children express a wish, or show an interest, before installing play equipment or garden toys: there is no point setting up goalposts if nobody in the family is interested in football.

ADVENTURE

Most children of this age love adventures, and a garden designed with hidden paths, secret shrub areas, and a few large rocks can become the setting for elaborate games of make-believe. The larger the area the better, but it should not be so large that children can become lost or frightened.

WATCHPOINTS

🌿 Always ensure that children feel safe in their garden. If they find an area frightening, such as a shadowy shrubbery, try to find a way of making it seem friendlier.
🌿 When children start on excavations, always keep a check on the position and depth of holes, and keep younger children away.

LEFT *A fun container garden which would be a certain winner as the children's entry in the local flower show (make sure the owner doesn't need the boots any more).*

GAMES IN THE GARDEN

Almost all children love playing games, whether on their own, in a twosome, or with a crowd of friends and family. There are lots of games that can be played in the garden, not all of which need a lawn or lots of room.

- A basketball net fixed to a house or garage wall can give hours of pleasure to aspiring basketball players.
- Laying paving slabs on the terrace or a side path that can be marked and used for hopscotch is very easy.
- An enlarged sandbox can be used for games when the bucket-and-spade brigade are in bed or occupied elsewhere.
- A table tennis table can be set up on any flat area of concrete, asphalt, or smooth paving.

CAMPSITES

Camping can involve simply putting up a tepee for an afternoon. At the other extreme, you could set up a tent for the summer and offer the chance to sleep out in the garden, with meals around a campfire. If a tent is to be erected for more than one day, it needs to be sited where it doesn't matter if the underlying grass gets damaged. Tents with integral groundsheets can be sited on sand, bark, or bare soil.

DIGGING HOLES

Some children love digging holes, and the deeper the better. This requires a spare area, and light, easily dug topsoil and subsoil. It could be a part of the vegetable garden between crops, as long as all holes are filled in once the ground is needed for growing plants.

GAMES ON GRASS

Even a small lawn can be used for game playing. Tetherball needs a relatively small circle, as does marbles. A crazy golf course can be set up in whatever space is available, including along grass paths and any side lawns. A soccer goal merely needs space in front to aim the ball and some tough plants that can survive being hit.

Larger, more regularly shaped areas are needed for baseball and volleyball, depending on the age and ability of the players. Short tennis and badminton need a 44 x 20ft (13.5 x 6.8m) rectangular area for the court, but will also need additional grass around the court for players to serve and run out. Wherever games are to be played, the lawn area needs to be surrounded by tough plants that are hardy enough to survive children rushing in among them to retrieve balls, and being hit by balls and the rackets and sticks of frustrated players.

BELOW *A children's lookout—an excellent alternative to a treehouse where there is no suitable tree available.*

FAMILY PETS

Your garden may also need to accommodate the family pets. Whatever the number and types of animals concerned, they need to be carefully considered when planning your garden. Lack of good planning can lead to disaster: the cat might use the sandbox as a litter tray, the rabbits might escape from their hutch and eat all your lettuces, and the dog might create brown circles on the lawn. With a little foresight, your garden can become a comfortable home for all your family pets.

Dogs can be great companions for all members of the family, but their needs will have to be accommodated within the garden. Make sure that the garden is escape-proof, with secure surrounding fences or walls and gates. This containment can be dual-purpose and keep small children safe as well. If you have a new puppy, make sure that the fence and gates will still be high enough to prevent escape when the dog is fully grown.

Bored dogs can become destructive and may start digging craters in a favorite rose bed or in a dearly loved children's garden, so there should be room for the dog to play and exercise, and areas to sit in both sun and shade. An outside kennel will give it a sheltered and shady place that is its own special territory within the garden.

No matter how often a dog is exercised, all dogs will on occasion use the garden as a toilet. Feces should be removed as soon as possible, and disposed of either in the household waste or in a garbage can sunk into a spare area of the garden. Unfortunately, females' urine tends to burn holes in the lawn, so they need to be trained to use a corner of the garden. Male dogs urinating on edible plants can be a health hazard; if the dog cannot be kept away from these areas, then you should fence off the vegetable garden or grow herbs and salad plants in raised beds.

Some dogs love water: Labradors will jump into any pond, however small, and can cause havoc with the carefully nurtured life in your wildlife pond. In a small garden it is probably a case of training the dog to keep out of the water, or installing a wall or pebble fountain instead.

CATS

Unlike dogs, cats are independent animals, living their own lives most of the time and condescending to join in our lives when they feel like it. Like dogs, they can get bored, and enjoy sharpening their claws, so give them their own personal scratching post rather than leaving them to remove the bark of a newly planted tree.

Cats will find their own exercise, but many of them love climbing, and children's treehouses might have been custom-made for cats. They spend much of their time sleeping, and prefer a warm area of paving in the sun, preferably where they won't be walked on by small feet.

They are clean animals and like to dig holes for their toilet arrangements, and cover them after use. This may not matter in the established parts of the garden, but it is a real nuisance if they choose the children's sandbox. The

LEFT *This attractive and unusual rabbit hutch can be moved around the garden to avoid damage to the grass. Children will also enjoy looking after chickens: they are relatively easy to care for and home-laid eggs are always a treat.*

🐾 A possibility for a larger garden would be a dovecote with resident mourning doves.

🐾 If you want free-range eggs, give your chickens the run of the garden during daytime, but be prepared to hunt for the eggs in the undergrowth.

🐾 It is impossible to keep cats in a garden unless you build a high wall around the whole boundary.

answer is to have a cover for the sandbox and to give the cat its own sand toilet elsewhere in the garden.

ABOVE *The family cat may be inclined to attack birds, so place a small bell on a cat collar to warn birds of the danger.*

As a special treat for your family cat, plant some plants for it to enjoy, like catmint (*see page 78*). This is a real favorite with cats and they will eat it, roll on it, and finally sleep in it. Plant a couple of plants to allow for damage, and you might find it necessary initially to fence off the plants to get them successfully established.

Cats and birds are not really compatible, so you may have to choose between attracting birds and accommodating the family cat. One proven method of keeping the two apart is to put a bell on the cat's collar to warn birds when it is on the prowl.

HAZARDS

🐾 Geese can become territorial and aggressive and may decide to keep everyone else out of the garden!

🐾 A guinea pig or rabbit run should have a wire mesh floor to prevent the animals from digging out and escaping.

🐾 Animal feces can be a health hazard, so make sure that animals do not foul play areas.

🐾 Family pets, especially dogs, can be jealous of a new baby, so keep a watch on your pet for the first few weeks to make sure that all is well.

RABBITS AND GUINEA PIGS

Rabbits and guinea pigs are easy to tame and like being handled by children; they are social animals and prefer to be kept in pairs. To avoid excessive breeding, ensure that you keep two females together, or keep a rabbit with a guinea pig, as they seem to enjoy sharing accommodation.

Both animals need housing that can stay outside in the summer, plus the protection of a shed or outbuilding in the winter. The hutch needs two compartments, one for sleeping and the other for feeding, and should be raised off the ground for ventilation. Place it where it is easily accessible and enjoys sun for at least part of the day. Both animals enjoy exercise and need a safe area in which to run. A portable run that can be moved around the lawn is better than a permanent enclosure.

TURTLES

Turtles are just great fun to watch as they slowly trundle over the garden or munch a lettuce leaf. They can be given the whole garden as their territory or be restricted to one area. A special house will provide shade from the sun and can be used for winter hibernation.

BIRDS

Chickens, ducks, and geese can all be kept as pets. Chickens, particularly bantams, make good pets for slightly older children, who will enjoy looking after them and collecting the eggs. They need hen coops to roost in at night for protection from animals, and enclosed runs that can be moved around the garden.

In a larger garden, there may be room to include a few ducks, preferably with their own duckpond, and even a few geese. The latter make excellent guard dogs.

PREPARING A PLAN—A SURVEY

To get the most out of your garden it is essential to plan the overall layout before making decisions on the details: that is, you should plan where the rose beds are to go before deciding on the list of roses to plant. Again, all members of the family can be involved in the planning process, from surveying the garden to working out the plan on paper. An involvement at this early stage should make everyone feel that this is their garden.

To create a well-designed garden you need to compose a series of linked "pictures", each with one of your chosen garden features at the center. Place each feature carefully so that it forms the center of the picture: a seat lined up with the path, a sundial in the exact center of a herb garden, a path leading to the trunk of an existing tree. You may want to improve your garden "pictures" by enhancing your features: the sundial may look better on a circle of paving; the seat might have a hedge behind it, or an arch over it; the tree trunk may need a seat or a patch of white flowers at its base.

SURVEYING YOUR GARDEN

The first step is to draw a plan of your garden. This may sound impossibly difficult, but in reality it is quite easy. You may already have an architect's plan that includes the garden; if so, you can copy it onto a fresh piece of paper. If no plan exists, then proceed through the following steps:

1. Draw a rough sketch of the house and garden on a piece of paper. Label each corner of the site and the corners of the house with a letter. If you have both a front and back garden, it is usually easier to make two plans.
2. Next you need to measure the garden accurately. Use a long measuring tape or yardstick and measure the length of each boundary of the garden, i.e. along a straight line between the points you have labeled on your plan.
3. Having measured all the boundaries, measure across the plot between opposite corners. These cross measurements are vital to be sure that you get the shape of the garden accurately recorded on your plan.
4. You will also need to measure the walls of the house that are adjacent to the garden. Start at a corner and check the positions of any windows and doors as you proceed. If there is a gap between the house and boundary, be sure to measure this accurately.
5. Existing garden features that you want to keep, for example established trees, need to be measured from one of the boundaries. Find the distance up the line and then, at right angles to the boundary line, measure the distance to the feature. Check the size of the tree trunk and the spread of the tree's branches, as these may affect how you use or plant the area next to the tree.

SITE ANALYSIS

While you are surveying, check other factors that may affect how you plan the area. Use a compass to find the position of north, which will help indicate which areas of the garden are sunny and which are shady. If cold winds are a problem, note any sheltered parts of the garden. You also need to look out of the garden to establish any good views that are to be kept and any ugly views that may need to be screened.

LEFT *You will probably be happy to keep some of the existing features in your garden survey.*

DRAWING UP THE PLAN

You now need to select a scale. The easiest method is to use the inches marked on your ruler, using either 1in to represent 1yd on the ground—a scale of 1:100—or 2in for every 1yd—a scale of 1:50. Start by drawing the longest boundary line to scale on a piece of graph paper, and mark the ends AB, as on your sketch. To find the next point, C, stretch a geometry compass along your ruler to the scale length of line AC, place the compass point on A, and draw an arc for C. Repeat the same process for line BC; where the compass arcs cross is point C.

Repeat this process for the other corners, and then plot the position of the house including the doors and windows. Finally, plot the existing features using your ruler to find the distance up the boundary line, and then the distance into the feature.

FUNCTIONAL PLAN

Once you have a scale drawing of your garden, you can start allocating areas for the various items on the family lists. Start with the terrace area near the house, making sure it is large enough, and then the lawn. Find a sunny spot for vegetables and for sitting areas. Allocate space for any children's dens or treehouses, and any private areas for teenagers. Decide on sizes and positions of flower beds. Check that the area where younger children will play with their toys is safe and in view of the house, and that they have somewhere to try out their first set of wheels. If a pond is on the list, then consider where it might be placed. Finally, take into account the various needs of your pets.

ABOVE *A new house where there has never been a garden gives you the ideal opportunity to create a space that suits your family, without having to undo other people's mistakes.*

WATCHPOINTS

🍃 Be sure to read and write down measurements carefully—6 and 9, and 4 and 7, are easily confused.
🍃 Select either feet or meters for your measurements, choosing whichever system you prefer. Using unfamiliar units may lead to problems.
🍃 Have one person in charge—too many surveyors will definitely spoil the plan.
🍃 Avoid wet and windy days—a tape measure blowing in the wind is impossible to use accurately, and it is very difficult to record details on wet paper.

To complete the plan, you need to consider how to link the various areas of the garden. Will access be across the lawn or will you need to put in some paths? If you are going to have paths, you need to decide whether you want them to be paved or grass, and whether the shape should be curved or straight.

A SUBURBAN GARDEN

Where the garden is of a reasonable size it may be possible to have separate features or areas for the different age groups in the family. The first thing to consider is the position and size of the terrace and then the shape of the lawn. Once these have been established, you can then start fitting in all the other features required.

This garden is a typical rectangular shape and lies to the southeast at the back of the house. It is relatively flat and surrounded by a 6ft (1.8m) high fence. In planning the garden it was decided to use circular shapes for most of the features in order to soften the strong, straight lines of the fence, and to allow for a curving path around the garden. The three existing trees were attractive, so the plan had to allow for their retention and continued growth.

It is important to have good views into the garden from the windows of the house; the pebble fountain has been placed directly in front of the kitchen window and the herb garden is clearly seen from the sitting room. The terrace leads directly onto the lawn to allow the younger children to play on both surfaces, and there is a sandbox readily

POINTS TO CONSIDER

🍂 Be careful to allow for the continuing growth of existing trees—check their ultimate height and spread in a reliable reference book.
🍂 Use simple shapes for features like the herb garden and then repeat the shape elsewhere in the garden.
🍂 Use paving materials which reflect the materials, or the color of the materials, used in building the house.

visible from the sitting room or the terrace. The sandbox can be turned into a planted area when no longer needed.

A path encircles the lawn and doubles as a mowing strip and as a track for tricycles, toy cars, and other vehicles. The path also leads into and around the herb garden with its central sundial. This could be for culinary herbs for the kitchen, or a collection of colored-leaved herbs like golden marjoram and purple sage, or a mixture of both. Many herbs attract bees, including winter savory, thyme, lavender, and hyssop, so in summer this area will be alive with the buzz of bees collecting nectar.

Part of the area at the far end of the garden is left semi-wild for school-age children to have a place of their own for exploration and adventure. There is room for a wildlife hide, a pond, and a clump of fruiting shrubs to provide food for birds in autumn and winter. In the corner is an attractive wooden swing, strong enough for most adults as well as children.

Space is left for several seats around the garden so that there are sitting areas in both sun and shade. There is a selection of planted areas, in sun and part shade, so if the parents are avid gardeners they can include many of their favorite plants. There is room for a child's garden and a locked shed for tools and chemicals.

LEFT *A well-made, sturdy swing in a corner of the garden, ready to give pleasure to all members of the family.*

The comfortable arbor
has a seat for older
members of the family to
enjoy peace and quiet and
watch the bees at work.

The vegetable garden
and compost heap are
surrounded by a low
fence with a gate. There
is a bed along the fence
for growing cordon and
espalier fruit.

A large central lawn
allows a clear view into
most of the garden and
lots of space for toys
and games.

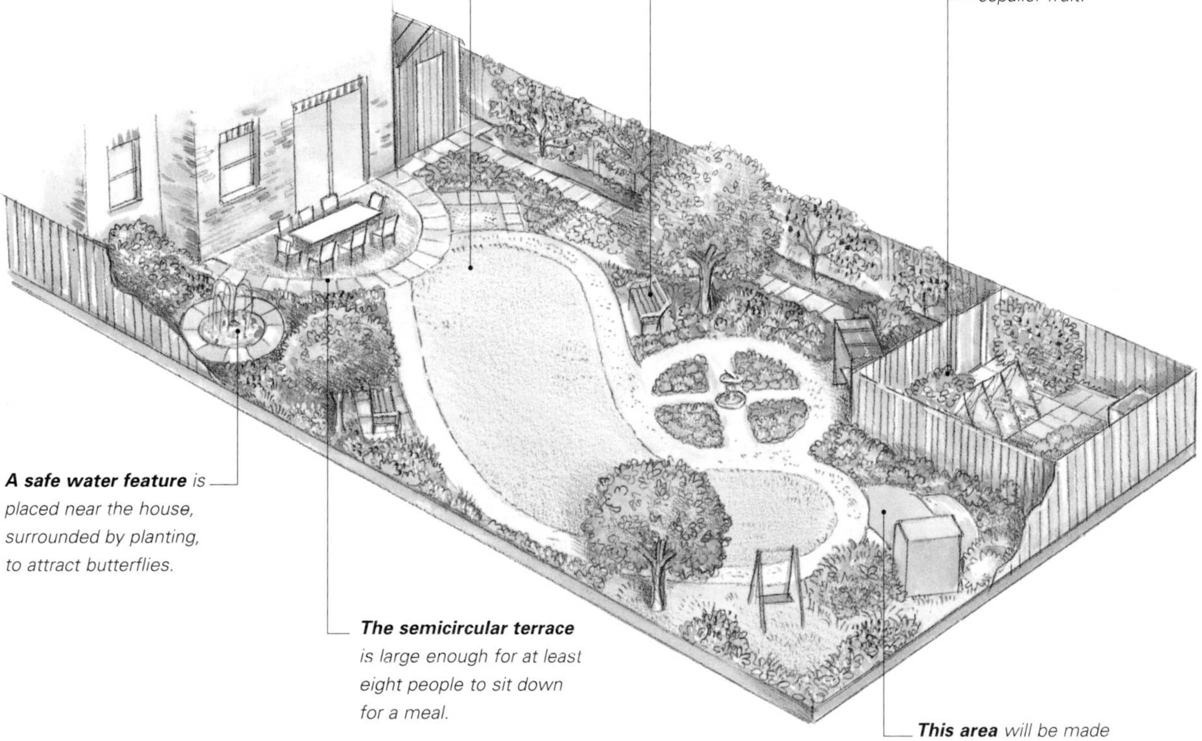

A safe water feature is
placed near the house,
surrounded by planting,
to attract butterflies.

The semicircular terrace
is large enough for at least
eight people to sit down
for a meal.

This area will be made
into a wildlife pond when
the younger children have
passed the age when a
pond is considered to be
a safety hazard.

ABOVE This is a plan for a medium-sized garden,
65ft x 39ft (20m x 12m), in a town where the
family has several children of different ages and a
dependent relative. There are three existing trees
and the house is to the northwest of the garden.

A SMALL COUNTRY GARDEN

A small garden requires more careful planning than a large one, especially when the requirements of all the family have to be taken into account. It is possible to create a very attractive and user-friendly garden which all the family can enjoy, although it may be necessary to eliminate some desirable features to achieve a workable solution. A relatively small garden can be subdivided to create separate "rooms", each of which can be designed for a specific use. These can be enclosed, with gated access if required.

This design is for an irregularly shaped garden at the end of a row of houses, with neighbors on one side. From the upstairs windows, there are views out over the country-side to the south and east. The garden is accessible through the conservatory, and also through the playroom.

The garden was designed to feature several distinct areas in order to accommodate the different needs of the various members of the family. It was also important to plan a really attractive view from the kitchen window, where the sink is sited.

THREE ROOMS

Three areas have been created, including a paved terrace, enclosed vegetable garden, and a lawn surrounded by beds and borders. The terrace area includes a small butterfly garden, also a herb garden, which has a pot of variegated lemon balm as a central feature. The terrace leads into both the other areas, with three steps up to the vegetable garden and a flat grass path to the lawn. The children can sit or play on the steps and the low wall but, while they are still young, a locked gate prevents them from entering the vegetable garden and causing havoc.

There is a bird bath situated in the middle of the vegetable garden, which can be seen both from the kitchen

ABOVE *In a family garden, one of the main considerations is the provision of an area that can host a table and chairs, so that meals can be enjoyed outside.*

and when standing on the terrace. As well as allowing plenty of room for the cultivation of fresh food for the kitchen, the vegetable garden also has a compost bin and a seat so that you can have a well-earned rest after digging the potatoes!

The lawn is clearly visible from the kitchen and the conservatory. Although it is not large enough for a game of football, there is enough space for a paddling pool and the younger children's toys. There is a range of planted areas around the lawn, both in the sun and partly in shade. One bed is planted with fruiting plants to attract birds. There is another small border that could be annexed by a child for his or her own garden. A sloping grass path leads up into the vegetable garden through a second gate.

An almost secret path runs the length of the hedge to allow access for hedge cutting and to the concealed cat's bathroom. Finally, tucked behind the corner of the house, there is a shed standing on a paved area for outside storage.

POINTS TO CONSIDER

🍃 Check whether the boundary walls or fences belong to you or your neighbor before embarking on any work.

🍃 Trellis forms a very attractive division in a small garden, taking up very little room and providing a great support for climbing plants.

🍃 Make the paved area as big as you can, so there is plenty of space for children to play and for the family to eat.

The low wall that separates the vegetable garden from the terrace is just the right height to provide extra seating when needed.

An extended terrace outside the playroom and kitchen has space for a table and four chairs, lots of toys, possibly a reclining chair or two, and a sandbox if desired.

A raised vegetable garden surrounded by a trellis planted with cordon fruit trees and blackberries.

There is room on the lawn for children to play; also for an inflatable paddling pool.

At the far side of the lawn a seat has been placed under the existing tree to provide a shady retreat. By adding a folding table, informal meals could be eaten here.

The trellis surrounding the vegetable area has lockable gates to keep children and animals out.

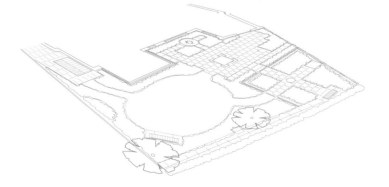

ABOVE *This is a plan for an irregularly shaped garden approximately 56ft x 33ft (17m x 10m). The house is the last on the street, and is separated from the adjoining field by a hedge. The family includes three small children and a cat.*

A VERY SMALL TOWN OR CITY GARDEN

Small gardens in the middle of towns or cities are often shaded by surrounding walls and houses, making it difficult for grass to grow really well. In such cases, it often makes better sense to pave the whole garden, leaving interesting spaces for planting. The garden can then be planned as a single outside room that includes as many functions and features as are feasible. The walls can be decorated with shade-loving climbers—flowering varieties to add color and evergreen species to enhance privacy.

This is a plan for a city garden, which originally consisted of a few concrete slabs and a scruffy lawn sloping up to the wooden shed against the end wall. Wooden fencing 6ft (1.8m) high marks the boundaries. A camellia grows against the fence to the east. The only access is through the house, using the French windows in the sitting room.

The new garden has been designed as an extension of the home, to provide a safe play space for small children and an interesting outlook from the house, with the provision for eating outside when the weather allows.

To eliminate the slope, the garden was divided into two levels (the upper and lower terraces) by a low wall with steps for access.

BELOW *For small garden owners who are determined to include a water feature, a wall fountain makes good use of the available space.*

POINTS TO CONSIDER

🍃 Small lawns can be difficult to mow and town gardens frequently suffer from a lot of shade, so it is often a good idea to remove the lawn completely and expand the terrace.

🍃 Pots of annuals add extra color to even the smallest garden and last from late spring until the first frosts.

🍃 When constructing a paved area, use small paving units to make the garden look larger.

Both terraces were paved with frostproof terracotta tiles, similar in size and color to those used in the sitting room and kitchen. They were laid on a slight slope to drain rainwater on to the planted areas to the west. The boundary fences followed the original slope, so planted areas were left on either side of the paving, which could be sloped to avoid creating a gap at the bottom of the fence.

UPPER AND LOWER TERRACES

The lower terrace was designed to create the maximum room for play equipment. A built sandbox was positioned in full view of the kitchen window and a bench placed in the shade of a small tree. There are two positions for the table and chairs—when they are by the water feature, an inflatable paddling pool will fit beside the sandbox on the lower terrace.

The upper terrace is designed to form an attractive view from the house, with a lion's head wall fountain providing a focal point. The shed is painted bright blue to provide a colorful contrast to the terra-cotta tiles. It is used for storage but it could be cleared and used as playhouse for the children when they are older. Containers of bedding plants provide extra color, with lobelia and marigolds in summer, and blue pansies and orange tulips in the spring.

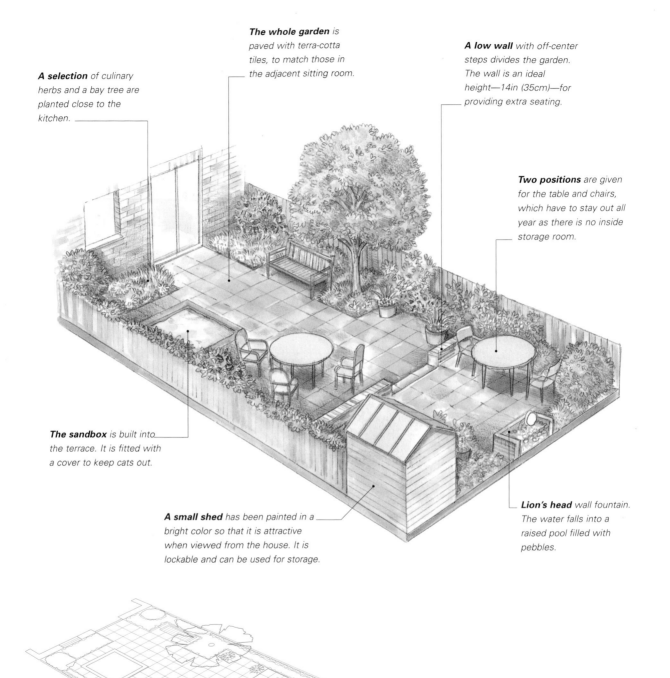

The whole garden is paved with terra-cotta tiles, to match those in the adjacent sitting room.

A low wall with off-center steps divides the garden. The wall is an ideal height—14in (35cm)—for providing extra seating.

A selection of culinary herbs and a bay tree are planted close to the kitchen.

Two positions are given for the table and chairs, which have to stay out all year as there is no inside storage room.

The sandbox is built into the terrace. It is fitted with a cover to keep cats out.

A small shed has been painted in a bright color so that it is attractive when viewed from the house. It is lockable and can be used for storage.

Lion's head wall fountain. The water falls into a raised pool filled with pebbles.

ABOVE This is a plan for a small, enclosed garden behind a terraced house in the middle of a large town or city. The garden is 28ft x 16ft (8.7m x 5m), and slopes slightly toward the house. The only access is through French windows from the house. The owners are a young couple with a two-year-old child and a new baby.

CREATING YOUR GARDEN

2

Now that you have decided on the type of garden you want, this is the time to make practical choices. Garden furniture comes in many shapes and sizes, and play items such as swings and jungle gyms need careful thought. Do you want a perfect lawn or one that will withstand football games? Do you prefer paving, brickwork, gravel, or decking, and would you like to include a wildlife pond or a wall fountain? This section will provide you with all the information you need to make the right choices for your garden.

LEFT *The creation of a relatively secluded area, where it is possible to relax in peace, might be a priority in a large, noisy household.*

GARDEN FURNITURE • CHOICES

①

TABLE AND CHAIRS

If you plan to eat out in the garden, you will need to consider a table and enough chairs to have one for each member of the family. Decide if you want them to stay out all year or whether they will be brought in either at night or for the winter. The choice is vast, but look for sturdy chairs that will not tip over when stood on by an active toddler.

If the family enjoys lying about in the garden, sunbathing, sleeping, or reading, then it may be worth investing in a couple of loungers. These can be simple aluminum folding recliners or more sophisticated sun loungers with adjustable feet and backs so that you can get really comfortable. They are made of wood, plastic, or resin, and some come with fitted cushions that can be removed.

②

BENCHES

These are seats for two or three people to sit on, and they are usually made of wood or metal. Metal seats can look very attractive, but wood is much warmer and softer to sit on. Perfect as seats placed around the garden in the sun or shade, they should be carefully sited to create attractive pictures—under a tree, at the end of a path, or beneath a rose arch, for example.

Picnic benches are rectangular tables with benches built in on either side. They are usually made of solid wood and can be heavy to lift and move. Lighter-weight versions and smaller models for children to use are now available. They can be used on the terrace but are more suitable for casual use, and are best placed in a long grass area.

CHOICE CHECKLIST	
❧ Consider comfort and durability first and buy the best quality that you can afford. ❧ All furniture needs to be checked regularly for loose	bolts and screws and cracked legs and seats. ❧ Plastic is generally cheap, light and easy to move about, but may discolor and become brittle with age.

CHOICE CHECKLIST	
❧ Traditional stone benches are elegant but expensive and uncomfortable to sit on. ❧ Wooden benches come in a range of prices and are comfortable, look natural,	and will last a long time if regularly oiled or painted. ❧ Painted metal can look attractive and is durable, but will need regular repainting and can be uncomfortable.

③

HAMMOCKS AND SWING SEATS

A hammock stretched out between two trees invites you to climb in and relax as it gently sways. Made in a variety of soft but strong materials, they are now available with either one or two supports for use when either a single tree or no other support is available. For young children, hammocks could form part of a make-believe game of pirates and shipwrecks, while older family members will simply enjoy the relaxing experience.

A more expensive, but extremely comfortable, alternative is a cushioned swing seat, which is much easier to get into and out of than a hammock, particularly for an older member of the family. Swing seats usually have a canopy at the top of the frame, so an added bonus is shade from the sun.

CHOICE CHECKLIST

❧ Most hammocks are made of rotproof materials which can be left outside all summer without damage.
❧ Check that there is adequate space for swinging without hitting anything.
❧ Hammocks require secure and strong fixtures and swing-seat frames need to be correctly anchored to the ground.

④

LOGS AS FURNITURE

There are lots of inexpensive or even free ways of furnishing a garden, particularly where children are concerned. A few large logs cut to the right length and stood upright are instant stools, and if a larger slab of wood is laid on three or four of the logs, you have a rustic table. A large log left lying on its side makes a comfortable child-height bench. If you are feeling imaginative, and have some carpentry skills, you could construct a table and some chairs … or even a treehouse!

If there are large smooth rocks, they can also be used as chairs and tables, but be sure they are set firmly into the ground. Remember that rocks will be slippery when wet, so discourage young children from climbing on them after rain.

CHOICE CHECKLIST

❧ Use hardwood logs where available as these take longer to rot than softwood.
❧ Check logs for loose splinters and remove any before placing in position.
❧ Logs will attract insects, so avoid using them if your children dislike creepy-crawlies (though these will provide a source of interest for some children).

PLAYING IN THE GARDEN • CHOICES

①

SWINGS AND SLIDES

A simple wooden swing or rubber tire suspended from a tree branch or frame is still a firm favorite with all age groups. Make the swing sturdy enough, and even adults may be found idly swinging backward and forward when no one is looking. Constructed swings can be made that have room for plants like honeysuckle to be planted over them to make a very attractive garden feature.

Slides come in a variety of materials, but safety remains a major consideration. A slide should have handrails at the top and high enough sides to prevent children falling out. The safest slide is one that follows the contours of a slope. Consider buying a plastic slide for a toddler and a larger slide for older children that will last for many years.

CHOICE CHECKLIST	
∽ Slides need a clear space at the bottom where children can land.	∽ Swings need space in front and behind to ensure that nobody gets hit when the swing is in motion.
∽ Wood looks more natural in the garden than the plastic alternatives.	

②

JUNGLE GYMS

Children love climbing, whether it is on ropes, ladders, rocks, or trees. A strong tree with plenty of low branches will make the perfect climbing spot, and nothing else is really necessary. If, however, you hang a rope ladder from one branch, a swing from another, and place a simple platform in a fork in the tree, you have a ready-made adventure playground. If you do not have a suitable tree, you will need some form of framework, metal or wood, to which ropes, rope ladders, scrambling nets, or solid ladders can be fixed. The same structure can be used to support a slide, a swing, and even a platform with a roof, which can be used as a playhouse. Never site a jungle gym on a hard surface: choose grass or lay a safety surface.

CHOICE CHECKLIST	
∽ Any climbing equipment needs clear space at the base for jumping off safely.	∽ Choose a system that allows attachments to be altered as children get older; for example, being able to change a baby swing for a rubber tire swing.
∽ Check all fittings and fixtures regularly for signs of wear.	

3

PLAYHOUSES

Playhouses, hideouts, treehouses, and dens are all spaces for children to use where they can enter their own world of make-believe. Where a more permanent dwelling is wanted, look for a structure that will be strong and big enough for several years of play. A well-built wooden house may be more expensive than a plastic one, but it will give years of pleasure. An ordinary garden shed, with the addition of a child-sized door and small windows, can make a dream cottage that can be returned to its original function when no longer needed. Playhouses are best as a permanent fixture in the garden, and can form an attractive picture. You could enhance the view by adding a garden around the sides or placing flower pots in front.

CHOICE CHECKLIST	
∽ The adjacent garden and pots could be planted by the user or users of the playhouse and be their special responsibility.	∽ Large cardboard boxes, suitably painted and with holes cut out for windows and doors, make great temporary houses and can be thrown away afterward.

4

FLOORING FOR PLAY SPACES

For toys that are put away at night, grass makes the perfect flooring as it is soft and resilient to play on. Where play equipment is to be fixed permanently, grass is less satisfactory as it tends to get worn and muddy. The grass may be difficult to mow and, if the play equipment is in shade, will not grow well. Sand is used in some children's playgrounds, because it is soft to fall on and can be used for digging, but more often nowadays you find a specially laid safety surface. For the garden, bark chippings are a good choice: they will provide a cushion on which to fall, and their natural dark color blends well with beds and borders. Another alternative is to lay an area of rubber safety tiles, which have the added advantage of being washable.

CHOICE CHECKLIST	
∽ There is a wide range of grades of bark chippings available. It is important to choose a nonsplintery bark for playgrounds—you may need professional advice.	∽ Before laying any surface, check that the soil beneath is well drained to prevent waterlogging. ∽ Rubber tiles are a good choice but can be expensive.

PAVING MATERIALS • CHOICES

❶

PAVING SLABS

Natural stone slabs are made from quarried sandstone, slate, or limestone. They look lovely but are expensive, heavy to handle and lay, and most can be slippery when wet.

Reconstituted stone slabs are precast slabs made from crushed stone mixed with a binding of cement; they come in a wide variety of shapes, colors, sizes, and finishes. All good garden centers have a selection on display, and many of the companies supplying the slabs have excellent catalogs that give instructions for laying them.

Finally, concrete slabs are strong, durable, and cheap but rather dull and uninteresting. If this is the only choice available or affordable, then add interest with an edging of paving blocks or bricks.

CHOICE CHECKLIST

❧ Select slabs to match materials already used in the garden or in the house.
❧ Ensure that all paved surfaces are laid to a minimum slope of 1 in 100

away from the house or garden walls.
❧ The level of the terrace should be at least 6in (15cm) below the water barrier membrane of the house.

❷

BRICK PAVERS AND PAVING BLOCKS

Brick pavers are clay bricks similar to house bricks but often thinner and without a recess on one side. They can be found to match the color of many house and walling bricks, and are most attractive in a garden. Available as both reclaimed and new, they are excellent for paths or detailing to concrete and paving slabs, but rather uncomfortable as the sole material for a terrace. They are also expensive and can be rather slippery when covered with moss.

Paving blocks are durable units, about the same size as a brick, made from clay or concrete. They are available in a wide range of colors and some unusual shapes, with either straight or beveled edges. Frequently used on drives, they are fairly expensive to buy and time-consuming to lay.

CHOICE CHECKLIST

❧ There are many different patterns for laying bricks— select the pattern most suitable for the area.
❧ Check that any bricks used for paving are

frostproof—bricks used in walls may not be and will break up in a cold winter.
❧ Large areas of bricks can look "busy" so break them up with larger paving units.

❸

DECKING

Wooden decking and tiles have been used for many years in countries with dry climates. Despite being slippery when wet, wooden tiles are now gaining in popularity as they tend to look softer and more natural in a garden setting than the stone alternatives. Decking can be used to replace a terrace, as a surround for a pond, or anywhere in the garden where you want a low platform.

Good decking is expensive but worth the cost; cheaper versions are rather splintery for knees and bare feet. Avoid mixing decking with other paving material such as stone slabs, as it can look rather untidy. The only surface material with which it associates well is loose stone, whether gravel, pebbles, stones, or even large rocks and boulders.

CHOICE CHECKLIST	
∞ Choose the best quality decking that you can afford.	∞ Decking is lightweight and ideal for roof gardens.
∞ Avoid laying decking on bare soil—use battens of treated timber as a support.	∞ You can use decking as an elegant method for covering up expanses of ugly concrete.

❹

GRAVEL AND CONCRETE

Gravel is by far the cheapest material to use for drives or garden paths and includes a wide range of small stones from angular chippings to rounded pea gravel. It is a useful material for less formal parts of the garden and combines well with rocks and water features. The finer the gravel, the easier it is to walk on, and there is a self-binding gravel which makes a compacted, hard-wearing surface. Gravel is not suitable for a terrace and should only be used for paths if there are no small children.

Concrete is often considered too utilitarian for a garden, but it makes a perfect, smooth bicycle track or hard play area. If used for a path, it will look much more attractive if given a brick or block-paving edging.

CHOICE CHECKLIST	
∞ Look at a range of gravel sizes and colors before making your selection.	∞ Concrete can be colored and can be laid with an extensive range of different finishes, including smooth, brushed, or exposed aggregate.
∞ Gravel can be laid on a water-permeable fabric or weed-barrier fabric to suppress weeds.	

WATER FEATURES · CHOICES

❶

PEBBLE FOUNTAINS

There are several different styles of pebble fountain but they all consist of a sunken reservoir containing water and a pump. The reservoir is covered with a lid or mesh on which are placed large pebbles. A jet of water rises out of the pebbles, and the water falls back through the stones and into the reservoir. In some versions, the jet comes up and over a millstone that sits on the pebbles.

Installing jets in paving is basically a more sophisticated version of the pebble fountain, where the lid supports paving rather than pebbles. Jets of water shoot up through the paving and then drain back through gaps into the reservoir. Children can run through the jets, and there is the potential to have a hidden switch to turn them on and off.

CHOICE CHECKLIST	
❧ An excellent choice where small children are concerned as there is no exposed body of water.	suitable for even the smallest of gardens.
❧ Available in a wide range of sizes and styles, and	❧ Include as large a reservoir as possible to avoid endless refilling.

❷

SHALLOW STREAM

A less obvious idea, but one ideal for children's games, is to create a water feature that is filled only when needed and left empty when not in use. A shallow indentation or ditch is excavated as part of the terrace, and then a hard surface material is laid. Small unit paving, blocks, and bricks are all suitable, but they must be properly laid with mortared joints, and the levels must be right. A hose can be used to fill the channel when a stream is wanted, and a temporary dam placed at the end of the channel can be removed when play has finished. The stream can double as a drainage channel for the terrace— but it is important to plan the stream as part of the pattern of the terraced area to ensure that it is visually appealing when empty.

CHOICE CHECKLIST	
❧ Safe except for very small children.	❧ Needs careful planning.
❧ Easy to maintain and keep clean.	❧ Allow a slight slope—at least 1 in 100—to ensure that the stream drains completely when not in use.
❧ Good value for paddling, boats, and water play.	

❸

WALL FOUNTAIN AND RAISED POND

This attractive feature comes in a wide variety of designs and prices, ranging from a simple jet falling into a basin to a series of elaborate jets falling into a large raised pool. Where the basin or pool is large enough, aquatic plants and fish may be introduced into the water. Choose according to site, preference, and budget.

The pond height needs to be a minimum of 14in (40cm), which will prevent small children or others from tripping over the edge and still allow everyone to view the pond easily. Up to 15in high, the edge of the pond can be used as a sitting area by adults and children. If there are very young children, select a wall fountain which falls into a high bowl fixed to the wall well out of reach.

CHOICE CHECKLIST	
❧ Ensure that there is a nearby water supply to allow regular refilling.	❧ It is possible to buy a kit which includes the pool, jets, and pump.
❧ Fountains can be very ornamental and give pleasure to all the family.	❧ Ensure that the pipe from the pool to the wall fountain is completely obscured.

❹

GROUND-LEVEL POOL

Ground-level pools, whether formal or informal, are the most popular of all water features, and will appeal to young and old alike. They give the opportunity to grow various water and bog plants, and will attract many kinds of wildlife.

They can be installed easily using a preformed shell or, more inexpensively, a rubber liner. Decide on the position for the pool and its shape, then dig out the soil to the required depth. Cover the base and sides with a layer of padding, then carefully fit the liner. Fill the pool with water so that the liner is fully stretched into the contours of the pool, then edge the pool with paving. This will hide the top of the pond liner and makes an attractive feature in its own right.

CHOICE CHECKLIST	
❧ A fountain can be added for extra interest, or even a waterfall.	❧ A method of controlling algae needs to be considered before selecting this type of water feature.
❧ Pools can be planted with a range of attractive water plants.	❧ Can be as small or large as space allows.

USE OF GRASS AREAS · CHOICES

❶

LUXURY LAWN

This is the perfect English lawn, with a smooth, velvety green sward and the typical stripes of precision mowing. It is the result of a mixture of fine grasses and close, regular mowing with a cylinder mower. It looks beautiful but needs very careful preparation and constant care and allows little or no wear. It is therefore not really suitable for a family garden unless one of the family is a lawn "fanatic," and would certainly not be the right choice if anyone wanted to play football or tennis or ride a bike on it. This is a lawn for admiring rather than using. For the highest-quality lawns, a mixture of Kentucky bluegrass, perennial ryegrass, and red fescue is the best mix for most of northern North America.

CHOICE CHECKLIST	
❧ Seed mixture should should contain Kentucky bluegrass, perennial ryegrass, and red fescue. ❧ Mow when grass reaches 2–3in (5–7cm) high.	❧ Mow as needed, usually once a week in summer. ❧ Scarify and feed the lawn each spring and reseed bare areas if, and when, they appear.

❷

UTILITY LAWN

This is a useful lawn for a family garden; fine grasses mixed with additional perennial ryegrass give a smooth, green sward that will take the pressures of everyone walking over it and the odd football game. The perennial ryegrass is quick to germinate and resistant to wear, but it will not tolerate being cut too short. There are enough fine grasses in the mixture to give the appearance of a neatly mown lawn.

Ground preparation is essential for a good-quality lawn. Ensure that all perennial weeds have been removed, and, if possible, leave the prepared soil for a few weeks before sowing, so that any remaining weed seeds have time to germinate. Spring is an ideal time to sow a new lawn; if you are not ready to sow then, wait until autumn.

CHOICE CHECKLIST	
❧ Seed mixture should be about 40% perennial ryegrass, 20% creeping red fescue, 20% Kentucky bluegrass, 20% Chewings fescue.	❧ Mow as needed, after grass reaches a height of 2–3in (5–7cm).

❸

PLAY AREAS

This grass area is intended for regular use, the hard wear of vigorous ball games, and being covered with paddling pools and tents, or more permanently with play equipment. The grass mixture may include a much larger proportion of perennial ryegrass which will put up with the continuous pressure of feet. The grass is cut at a higher level and is difficult to keep looking well groomed.

Weeds may be a problem as the higher level of mowing allows ground-hugging plants like plantains, dandelions, and buttercups to grow undisturbed. Hand weeding or use of a selective weedkiller may be needed to keep them under control. When the area gets damaged it is very easy to re-seed as perennial ryegrass germinates very rapidly.

CHOICE CHECKLIST

❧ Try a seed mixture of 60% perennial rye grass, 25% tall fescue, 15% red fescue, or a mix with rough-stalked and Kentucky bluegrass added.
❧ Mow when the grass has reached 3in (7cm) high.

❧ Check for toys and remove before mowing as they can seriously damage mower blades.

❹

WILD FLOWER MEADOW

A meadow is a lovely idea but not easy to establish, because the grass tends to take over from the wild flowers. Choose an area where the topsoil is poor, because this will inhibit grass growth and give the wild flowers a chance to get established. Sow seeds of wild flowers with the existing grasses, or plant small plants (plugs) once the area is established. Cut with a rotary mower set at the highest level.

An alternative is to plant spring-flowering bulbs in the grass and leave them to naturalize. The area is mown in the late autumn and then left for the bulbs to appear in spring. The first mowing is done when the bulbs have died down. Seed mixtures can include a wide range of grasses, but not perennial ryegrass because it is much too vigorous.

CHOICE CHECKLIST

❧ Try a mix with grasses that are native to the area. Usually a meadow seed mix contains wild flowers with bents and fescues.
❧ For a succession of

blooms add crocus, daffodils, summer snowflake, fritillaria, and lilies. Care should be taken to mow when the plants are not flowering and to let the bulb foliage mature.

GARDEN BASICS

A new garden will almost certainly need some plants, and most of these may need to be purchased from a suitable supplier. Try to decide what you want before you go, using the plant directory on pages 64 to 99 to tell you which plants will be suitable for your garden. If you buy on impulse, you risk being disappointed when your sun-loving purchase fails to flourish in your shady garden.

Plants are available for sale in a variety of outlets, from specialist nurseries and garden centers to the local greengrocer, market stall, or garage. Nurseries usually grow and sell their own plants, but, although the staff are usually very knowledgeable and helpful about the plants they grow, they may not have all the plants you are seeking. Most garden centers carry a whole range of plants from large conifers to tiny alpines, and some will look for plants from other sources when requested. When making a list of the plants you want, always put down the Latin name because most nurseries and garden centers arrange their plants alphabetically by their Latin names.

The best time to plant trees, shrubs, and roses is in the dormant season in very early spring; this is also a good time to buy. Herbaceous plants and conifers, by contrast, are best bought and planted in early autumn or spring.

Although plants in containers can be planted at any time of the year, the top buying and planting season is Easter to early summer. Planting in the spring means that the plant will go into soil that is beginning to warm up; and, if kept well watered in dry periods, it should start to grow immediately and continue to grow all summer.

BUYING BULBS

Spring-flowering bulbs are usually planted in September and October, although they are on sale from late August onward. Garden centers carry a good range of standard varieties at reasonable prices, but a much wider range can be found through mail-order specialty bulb companies. Their catalogs come out in midsummer, and orders are sent out in August and September. Summer- and autumn-flowering bulbs are usually planted in the spring and are available for sale in the late winter. Always check the planting time when buying bulbs, because they are best planted as soon as possible after buying or delivery.

BUYING SEEDS

Seeds can be bought in garden centers from late winter onward for early spring sowing. Again, there are specialty seed firms that supply a much wider range of seeds, but you need to allow time for your order to be processed and there may be a charge for delivery. The number of seeds in a packet varies widely, but it is often printed on the packet or in the seed catalog, so you can check that a packet contains enough seeds before you buy. Seeds will keep for some time but need to be stored in a dark, dry place. Some seeds come in foil inner packets which allow easier resealing when necessary. These packets are particularly useful with some salad crops that are to be sown in succession. If a seed packet contains more than you need, share them with your friends rather than keeping them until the next year.

LEFT *With careful advance planning, you can ensure color in the garden in every season.*

🌺 Make a list and set yourself a budget before buying plants—it is very easy to get carried away when faced with a garden center full of lots of lovely plants!

🌺 Many nurseries have reference books available for customers' use, so if you see a plant that looks fascinating but you know nothing about it, look it up before buying.

🌺 Always check that the soil, light, and moisture requirements of the plants you buy match the conditions in your garden. It is very, very easy to see an attractive plant but not note that it requires an acid soil and deep shade while you have a limey garden in full sunlight.

🌺 Do not be seduced by plants in flower. The best plant to buy is one that is growing vigorously, and that is usually before it is in flower. However, if you are looking for a particular color within a species, it is safest to choose a plant whose flowers are out, otherwise you could get a disappointing surprise.

🌺 Look for lots of healthy shoots and young leaves about to open. Dead leaves and shoots indicate a plant that is under stress.

TECHNIQUE   SELECTING PLANTS IN CONTAINERS

1 The soil in the container must be moist without being waterlogged. If it is excessively wet, the roots may have started to rot. If it has dried out, the plant may die.

2 If moss is present on the surface of the soil, this indicates that the plant has been neglected and has been in the pot too long.

3 Check that masses of roots are not protruding out of the container's drainage holes. This indicates that the plant is pot bound. Plants seldom recover fully if the roots are excessively matted.

4 Check that the plant has not been recently potted up for a quick sale. Reputable suppliers will not try to cheat potential customers, but this state often cannot be detected until the plant is planted. Make sure too that the plant is clearly labelled.

PROPAGATING PLANTS

If you are given plants, check that there are no signs of disease before you plant them in your garden. If you are given cuttings, keep them in water in a plastic bag until you are ready to handle them, then dip the stem of each cutting in hormone rooting powder or liquid, and plant in some cutting soil. Water them gently. You can put quite a few cuttings into one pot. Cover them with a plastic bag (sealed round the pot with a rubber band), which forms a cocoon over the plants to keep the moisture in. The bag must not touch the leaves of the cuttings, or they will turn brown and drop off. If your cuttings start to go moldy, then they are probably too damp: you need to clear the accumulated moisture off the inside of the bag at regular intervals.

If you have a friend with a herbaceous plant that needs dividing, this is an excellent way to add to your own garden. The plant needs to be dug up carefully, by inserting two garden forks, back to back, into the center of the clump, gently pulling the plant in half. The center of the plant will often be woody, so the division of the plant should be continued until sufficient pieces have been removed from the outside. The center should be discarded, and the outside pieces are then ready for replanting.

CARE AND MAINTENANCE

*T**he whole idea of this book is to keep garden maintenance to a minimum to allow all members of the family to enjoy the garden. However, plants are living organisms and will need a little help to keep them alive and well. The secret to a healthy garden is a good humus-rich soil and plants that have been selected for the specific soil, moisture, and sunlight conditions found in the bed in which they are planted. Strong growing plants are less likely to succumb to the various pests and diseases commonly affecting garden plants.*

Whichever type of lawn or grass area you decide to include in your garden, it will require regular maintenance. Wild flower meadows may need mowing only twice a year and should never be fed, but a quality lawn needs spiking, feeding, as well as regular mowing.

One of the more common problems suffered by lawns in family gardens is the grass dying in small areas—frequent games of football, or leaving a paddling pool too long in one place, are the quickest ways to end up with bald patches on the lawn.

WILD FLOWER MEADOWS

However small the garden, if there is room for a lawn, then it is worth keeping part of the grass area as a wild flower meadow. The grass is left uncut in spring to allow other plants, such as daisies, asters, yarrow, boneset, and other wild flowers to grow. Children and adults alike will enjoy this area. Many of these flowers are also useful caterpillar plants and will help to attract butterflies into your garden. However, if anyone in the family is a hay fever sufferer, a wild flower meadow may not be a good idea.

TECHNIQUE   **REPAIRING BARE PATCHES IN THE LAWN**

1 Remove the dead grass and gently fork the affected area using a hand or garden fork, depending on the size of the area.

2 Rake the surface of the soil and remove any debris, checking that the surface of the soil is level with the surrounding grass. Add additional screened topsoil if needed.

3 Rake to form a fine seed bed and sow grass seed at 1oz per sq yd (30g per sq. m). See pages 42 and 43.

4 Cover the seed with a thin layer of screened soil and press down with a board.

5 Water with a fine head on a hose or watering can, being careful not to disturb the seed.

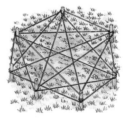

6 Protect from children and birds with crossed strands of rope twine.

1 Allocate a minimum space of 39 x 39in (1 x 1m) for the compost heap. A concrete or paved base makes it easier to remove the compost, but level, compacted soil is just as good, and also retains heat.

2 Make a bunker with wooden or brick sides and an open front. Place hedge clippings, cabbage leaves, or other coarse material at the bottom of the heap to allow air to get in and help the decaying process.

3 Place a layer of mixed garden waste on the heap; kitchen vegetable waste, lawn clippings, annual weeds, dead leaves, and flower heads can all be included, but avoid any plants containing invasive seeds.

4 Add some soil to the heap if none is present in the garden waste; also a little nitrogen-rich fertilizer (both encourage bacteria). Water the heap in dry weather.

5 Keep adding layers of vegetable waste, soil, and fertilizer until the heap is about 39in (1m) high. Cover with some extra soil and, in cold weather, with newspaper or leaves.

6 After 6–12 weeks you should have a brown crumbly compost. Remove the top and use as the base of the next compost heap; use the rest on the garden.

Some of these plants will occur naturally and some can be planted, including oxeye daisies, asters, cowslips, lilies, and harebells.

The area needs to be cut after the flowers are over: the grass can then be left to grow and should be mown only once a month to the end of autumn. This longer grass is softer to sit on and is perfect for picnics and campsites.

GRASS PATHS

Mown grass paths are a sensible, low-cost choice of path for less formal areas of the garden and for any path that is not used all the time. Use the utility lawn grass mixture *(see page 42)* and mow when the main lawn is mown. They need to be planned to be wide enough to allow easy access around the garden and to make mowing easy.

(see page 42)

HINTS AND TIPS

🌢 In the first year after planting, all plants will need regular watering during dry periods.
🌢 A check needs to be kept for weeds and these removed as soon as they appear, to avoid becoming a problem.
🌢 Deadhead flowers, as this usually results in more vigorous plant growth as well as making the plant look more attractive.
🌢 Most plants will benefit from an annual feed in the spring with a balanced fertilizer containing equal amounts of nitrogen, phosphates, and potassium.
🌢 An annual mulch of composted organic matter applied to the surface of the soil will keep the soil rich in humus, which is formed as the organic matter breaks down in the soil. The best source of this is garden-made compost from the compost heap.

SAFETY IN THE GARDEN

Family gardens should be, first and foremost, spaces in which the whole family can relax and enjoy themselves. For parents to be fully relaxed, they need to be certain that their children are safe and that they have guarded against all possible dangers. However, the need for safety will vary with the age of the children using the garden, and will change as children grow older.

A totally safe garden would be a space surrounded by high smooth walls and with a floor of washable rubber tiles on which were placed a few plastic toys. This might be fine for babies and toddlers, but would be a sterile desert to an adventurous older child. At the other extreme, a garden with no boundaries, deep pools of water with steep drops into fast-flowing streams, uneven, slippery paving, lots of poisonous plants, and an old greenhouse with rotten glazing bars and broken glass is a gloriously exciting place but a potential danger for every member of the family.

So how safe should your garden be? Look at what might constitute specific dangers for members of your family and then consider how to minimize those dangers. Get the older members of the family to do a risk assessment of your garden, as this will get them to appreciate the dangers for themselves and make them aware of how to avoid any potential problems.

BELOW *The flush edge to this relatively deep pool would be unsafe for small children.*

POINTS TO CONSIDER

RISK ASSESSMENT
Risk assessment means taking a potential hazard and looking at it in terms of the following:

🐾 How likely is it to cause an accident?
—High chance /some chance /low chance
🐾 How serious would the effect be?
—Death /serious injury /slight injury
🐾 What could be done to minimize the risk?
—If there is a high chance of a serious accident and there is a way of minimizing the risk, then this should be done.

Examples of garden pitfalls for an active two-year-old include the following:

Easily opened gate to road
🐾 High chance of running out into road and traffic.
Action—Replace gate immediately.

Open pond on terrace
🐾 High chance of slipping and falling in.
🐾 Possibility of drowning.
🐾 Could fence pond (unsightly), watch child constantly (not realistic), or replace pond with paving.
Action—Replace pond with paving.

Mildly poisonous aquilegia in front of border
🐾 No bright berries, so low chance of child being attracted to eating the plant.
🐾 Would cause stomach ache if eaten, but this is not dangerous.
Action—Dig up aquilegia and replant in middle or back of border.

WATCHPOINTS

RISKS FOR CHILDREN

Children have little sense of danger and are therefore most vulnerable to accidents, so while they are small there are a number of things you can do to make the garden safer.

🌿 Fence or remove open water—small children can drown in a few inches of water.

🌿 Ensure that children are always visible when playing in the garden by avoiding features that obscure parts of the view.

🌿 Check for poisonous plants—some children put everything into their mouths, and older children may mistake poisonous fruit for cherries or blackcurrants. Remove all very poisonous plants (*see entries on pages 104 to 107 of the plant directory*).

🌿 Check on plants that can cause skin rashes and allergies and decide whether to remove any present in the garden (*see entries on pages 100 and 101 of the directory*).

🌿 Position play equipment carefully so that children on swings cannot hit anything or anybody; and ensure that slides have protected tops. Always carefully follow the manufacturer's instructions for assembly and anchorage.

🌿 Select soft material for the base of play equipment, either grass, bark, mulch, sand, or rubber tiles, so that if a child falls the result is not too serious.

RISKS FOR ALL THE FAMILY

There are some potential hazards in a garden that might be dangerous for any family member, whatever their age and agility, and care needs to be taken with the following:

🌿 Avoid sharp objects—check for possible dangers like broken glass and projecting edges in greenhouses; ground-floor windows that open onto paths and terraces; sharp corners of coping on walls.

🌿 Cover tops of plant stakes and bamboo poles with rubber tips to avoid jabbing eyes or limbs when gardening.

🌿 Consider the position of plants with sharp thorns or prickles (*see entries on pages 102 and 103 of the directory*) and remove any of these plants that are adjacent to paths and children's play areas.

🌿 Create sitting and playing areas in shade to prevent sunburn.

🌿 Check and relay uneven and broken paving—this is dangerous to all members of the family but particularly the very young and the elderly.

🌿 Ensure that all garden chemicals and tools are kept in a locked shed and that the key is accessible only to responsible members of the family.

🌿 Have a well-equipped first aid kit in the house and be sure that all members of the family know where it is kept.

🌿 Post emergency telephone numbers near the phone.

ELECTRICITY

There are obvious dangers in using electricity in the garden, so take special care with equipment and electrically operated garden features, such as pumps on fountains.

🌿 All garden supplies must be fitted with a circuit breaker. Seek advice from a qualified electrician.

🌿 All electric cables must be shielded to protect from accidental damage.

🌿 Carry out regular checks on all electrical equipment, and replace any worn or damaged parts.

THE CARE AND USE OF TOOLS

Always put garden tools away after use in a locked shed, and note these other points about their safe use:

🌿 Learn how to dig properly to avoid injuring your back, and teach children to do the same.

🌿 When using tools, always place them so that they are safe, e.g. do not leave a rake with its teeth facing upward.

USE AND STORAGE OF CHEMICALS

Most of us would probably prefer not to use any chemicals in the garden, but they are useful aids and frequently there will be a few garden chemicals that need storing in your lockable garden shed. Here are a few additional rules:

🌿 Always read the instructions and follow them.

🌿 Never remove or destroy labels.

🌿 Never change containers, e.g. never pour weedkiller into an old soda bottle.

🌿 Never keep made-up solutions for use later.

🌿 Safely dispose of out-of-date or unused chemicals—contact your local authority for disposal advice.

🌿 Buy chemicals only when you are sure you need them and use them immediately.

PLANTING THE FAMILY GARDEN

In a small garden, plant trees, shrubs, climbers, and some of the tougher border plants that everybody can enjoy, and then add extra, perhaps more exciting, plants when the children have grown up and left home. Using child-resistant plants does not mean missing out on color and interest—there are lots of lovely plants that are tough and easy to grow, which are detailed in the plant directory, and in the star plants box on the facing page.

The most frequently made mistake in tree selection is choosing too large a tree so that, just as it matures into a really lovely specimen, it grows too large and has to be

chopped down or pruned back. Trees should offer year-round interest if possible, or at least an extended season of interest. In the plant directory there are 12 trees that are selected as being easy to grow, including *Sorbus* 'Joseph Rock'. You can buy trees in a variety of sizes from small seedlings to semi-mature "giants." The best size for a family garden is a 3½–4in (9–10cm) caliper standard tree. The 3½–4in measurement is the diameter of the trunk one foot above the ground, and standard means that the tree will have a clear trunk of 6ft (1.8m) and a well-formed, branching head.

"Bare root" trees are lifted without any soil in the autumn and winter; they should be planted only between late autumn and spring. "Container-grown" trees have been grown in a container and are more expensive; these can be planted all year but will need very careful handling and watering if planted in summer.

LEFT *Plant scented roses to fill the garden with perfume. This attractive planting teams them with alchemilla and geraniums.*

| PROJECT | PLANTING A CLIMBER AGAINST A FENCE |

1 Select the position for the climber, perhaps in the middle of a fencing panel or in between panels. Dig a hole 15in (38cm) away from the fence, slightly wider and deeper than the root ball of the climber.

2 Place the container in the hole to check that it is big enough. Fork over the base of the hole and mix in some well-rotted compost. In dry weather, fill the hole with water and let it drain away before planting.

3 Adding water to the hole before planting will ensure that the plant has moisture at its roots. Place the root ball in the hole and fill the gaps with topsoil, making sure that the soil is firmed in.

4 Push a bamboo cane firmly into the soil behind the climber to support the plant and guide it into position. Tie the shoots of the climber loosely to the cane. Water after planting and regularly during the first year.

PROJECT — PLANTING A BARE ROOT TREE

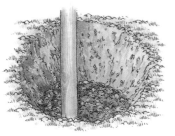

1 Select a site for your new tree and place a large bamboo cane in the ground to represent the tree. Look at the cane from all parts of the garden and the house to check that the site is correct. Dig a hole roughly 2 x 2 x 2ft (60 x 60 x 60cm), checking that it is large enough to contain the tree roots fully spread out and extra compost at the hole base.

2 Break up the sides and base of the hole by forking before planting to ensure adequate drainage. A newly planted tree requires plenty of water to get it established, but you don't want your tree to be saturated, so drainage is important.

3 Drive the stake in firmly near the center of the hole so that at least 18in (45cm) of the stake is in the ground and it feels absolutely firm. Position it so that when the tree is placed centrally in the hole the stake will be on the windward side of the tree. Add compost to the soil in the base of the hole.

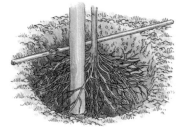

4 Hold the tree in the hole so that the junction of the roots and trunk of the tree is level with the top of the hole. Gradually fill the hole with soil and compost, making sure that the earth is firmed well, leaving no air gaps.

5 Tie the tree to the stake at the top and bottom using tree ties (if using a buckled tie make sure the buckle is on the stake and not the tree). The top tie should be nailed to the stake to prevent it slipping down. Water well and then cover the bare soil with 3in (75mm) of bark mulch.

6 Check the tree regularly to see that the stake is not rubbing the tree, and water frequently in dry periods in the first year. The tree ties will need loosening after the first growing season and the stake removing as soon as the tree is growing well—usually after three years. Mulch as needed.

SHRUBS AND HEDGES

Shrubs, particularly evergreen ones, give permanent structure to our gardens as a background to borders, as hedges (both formal and informal), as ground cover, and ornamentally as part of a mixed border. Most gardens include a hedge as a boundary, to divide up the garden, or as patterning. A hedge is a row of shrubs planted closely to create a uniform texture; it can be a single or double row. Most shrubs can be used as hedging; some are included in the plant directory *(pages 82 to 85)*.

STAR PLANTS

Some of the best all-round plants for a family garden are:

- *Clematis montana*
- *Hemerocallis* hybrids
- *Malus hupehensis*
- *Penstemon barbatus*
- *Rosa* 'Flower Carpet'
- *Rosa* 'New Dawn'
- *Viburnum tinus*

CHILDREN'S GARDENS

All children should be given the opportunity to grow plants, whether in a flower pot on the windowsill, in a half barrel on the terrace, or in their own garden. Watching a seed germinate and send out roots and shoots is to watch one of life's wonders, and almost all small children can be encouraged to sow a few seeds.

Start by letting children sow seeds in a pot. Mustard and cress are the quickest seeds to grow, being ready for cutting just two weeks after sowing. Beans are fun, as the unfurling leaves are huge; the resulting bean plant can either be left to grow in the pot or planted out in the garden to produce beans. Another favorite use of flower pots is to have a competition among family members to grow the tallest sunflower. Herbs such as parsley and dill are also useful starter plants for flower pot growing.

CAPTURING THEIR IMAGINATION

Almost anything can be used as a container—a growing-bag, an old tire, old shoes, and discarded toys. Whatever container is selected, it must have drainage holes in the base. Once they have grown plants in containers, children may want to have their own patch of garden to try out their new gardening skills and planting ideas.

Children should be given an area in which the soil is relatively easy to dig and in which their plants are likely to thrive. An area of heavy clay soil in deep shade will prove

RIGHT *Strawberry plants are a real winner because they are easy to grow and the fruits are delicious to eat.*

1 Place some broken crocks or stones in the bottom of the container for drainage, and fill the container with fresh planting soil to within 4in (10 cm) of the top.

2 Remove three nicotianas carefully from their pots, and place them close together in the center of the pot. Press into the soil, adding extra soil between the three plants.

3 Place five petunias equally around the center plants. Press into the soil, adding extra soil between the petunias and the nicotiana.

4 Place five lobelia and five alyssum alternately around the edge of the pot, and press into the soil. Adjust all the plants to allow equal spacing and then add extra soil. Water with a fine head on a hose or watering can.

PROJECT   PETUNIA PIG

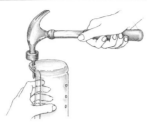

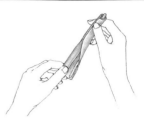

1 Cut an opening in one side of a juice or water bottle large enough to hold five plants, and use a hammer and nails to punch drainage holes in the side of the bottle opposite the opening.

2 Punch a hole in the back of the pig to attach the tail. Cut a piece of felt 4in (10cm) square and then cut it diagonally to make two triangles for the ears. Fold the triangles in half and glue the bottoms together to form the ears. Glue the ears to the bottle.

3 Cut a 2 x 6in (5 x 15cm) piece of felt and wrap it around a pipe cleaner or wire to make the tail. Glue the long edge of the felt to hold it firm. When the glue is dry, coil the tail around a pencil before pushing the end through the tail hole in the bottle. Fix by twisting the end of the tail into a knot.

4 Fill the pig with potting soil, starting with the head and making sure to pack it in well with no large air gaps.

5 Place four corks to form legs and make sure that the pig is steady on its legs before gluing the corks into position. Draw two eyes on the head of the bottle with a black marker pen

6 Plant the pig with petunias, and water well. Place in a sunny position and water every few days. If you haven't any petunias, any other small plants can be used. You could try sowing grass seeds in the back of the pig; cut your green pig's coat regularly.

daunting to even the most determined young gardener. Assistance from an older member of the family in preparing the soil by digging or cultivating it and in adding plenty of organic matter will help to get the young enthusiast off to a good start.

Encourage children to plan the garden rather than just scatter seeds everywhere. If they have started with container gardening, they may already have strong ideas about the plants they wish to grow. It is their garden, so let them plant every color together and decorate the garden with whatever they fancy—shells, lengths of wood, plastic toys. Stop a child from expressing their ideas and you may stop them from getting pleasure from the garden. The easiest plants to start with are hardy annuals.

STAR PLANTS

These are some of the best plants for children to grow:

- *Aquilegia vulgaris* (columbine)
- *Calendula officinalis* (marigold)
- *Eschscholzia californica* (Californian poppy)
- *Helianthus annuus* (sunflower)
- *Limnanthes douglasii* (poached egg plant)
- *Nigella damascena* (love-in-a-mist)
- *Tropaeolum majus* (nasturtium)
- *Viola* x *wittrockiana* (pansy)
- Carrots
- Bulbs

WILDLIFE IN THE GARDEN

*M*ost *people are fascinated by watching wildlife, whether it is bees busily collecting nectar and pollen, a friendly robin sitting on the fence, or frogs, toads, and other watery friends enjoying the garden pond. All of these creatures are a source of endless entertainment and all can be encouraged to come into your garden.*

There are hundreds of different species of bee living in North America. All of them visit plants to feed on the nectar and collect pollen to feed their young. If you want bees buzzing around your garden, then include some of the plants listed below in your beds and borders. Bees can be seen out foraging almost all year, particularly on warm, sunny days, so plant a range of bee plants that will flower in various different seasons.

Butterflies can be attracted into the garden by planting the plants that they are known to visit for nectar. Some of the best butterfly plants are listed below; these can be planted throughout the garden or grouped together to create a butterfly border. Most butterflies are active from mid- to late summer, coinciding with the school summer holidays, and a butterfly bed would make an interesting project for children to plant and maintain themselves.

STAR PLANTS

These are some of the best garden plants for attracting butterflies:

- *Aster novi-belgii*
- *Buddleja davidii*
- *Centranthus ruber*
- *Echinops ritro*
- *Eupatorium*
- *Hebe* 'Autumn Glory'
- *Origanum laevigatum* 'Herrenhausen'
- *Sedum spectabile*
- *Solidago canadensis*

Listed here are the best garden plants for attracting bees:

- *Borago officinalis*
- *Cotoneaster horizontalis*
- *Hyssopus officinalis*
- *Lavandula angustifolia*
- *Nepeta* x *faassenii*
- *Satureja montana*
- *Ulex europaeus*
- *Veronica spicata*

PROJECT — MAKING A TEMPORARY BIRD BLIND

1 Choose a sheltered part of the garden close to the pond and drive four 7ft (2.1m) posts into the ground to form a 4ft (1.2m) square. Secure four cross pieces to the top of the uprights, to form a square.

2 Create a viewing slit on the side of the blind next to the pond by nailing two cross pieces to the uprights. Nail two pieces of wood vertically between these two horizontals to leave a gap 20in (50cm) wide.

3 Fix sheets of black polythene to the top and three sides of the structure, cutting out a 8 x 20in (20 x 50cm) viewing slit. The side away from the viewing slit should be left uncovered for entry.

4 Camouflage the top and sides of the hide with leafy branches or other foliage. If you use branches of willow or poplar these may root and produce more permanent green cover for your blind.

1 Choose a warm, sheltered part of the garden for the border, which needs to be approximately 8ft (2.4m) wide and 6ft (2m) deep. Dig the area with a spade to remove any weeds.

2 Spread a thin layer of compost or organic matter over the soil and fork it into the surface.

3 Place a buddleja at the center back of the border, allowing 3ft 3in (1m) space around it, and then place a solidago and echinops on either side, allowing 2ft (60cm) spacing. When you are satisfied with the spacing, plant the three plants.

4 Now place a hebe and a caryopteris on either side and in front of the buddleja, then add two origanums, one at each end of the middle row, allowing 2ft (60cm) spacing for each of the plants. When you are happy with their positions, plant them carefully.

5 Next plant the front row. Place a sedum in the center, with two erigeron on one side and two asters on the other. All five plants need 18in (45cm) spacing. Make sure that the plants are 9in (23cm) from the front of the border, then plant carefully.

6 Add annuals such as French marigolds, alyssum, and scabious in any gaps in the bed for the first year. Water all the plants thoroughly. In future years when the other plants have started to spread, you may not need to add any annuals.

BIRDS IN THE GARDEN

There are lots of different ways to attract birds to the garden. Rather than planting a specific area for birds, include plants that provide food or nesting material throughout the garden. A source of water can be provided by a bird bath or a water feature, but make sure that there is somewhere flat to perch—a stone in the water is ideal.

Almost all gardens will provide some nesting materials, but you can help by leaving piles of leaves and twigs in the spring and even hanging nets of straw from branches. You could erect a birdbox and hope that a pair of nesting birds will take up residence.

RIGHT *A small butterfly collecting nectar from the flowers of* Aster novi-belgii.

VEGETABLES, HERBS, AND FRUIT

*F**reshly picked beans and new potatoes from your own garden are a real delight and are often considered an essential part of the family garden. Indeed, some family gardens are used entirely for the production of food to feed the family.*

Whether or not you grow vegetables depends on whether there is a family member who enjoys the work involved. Any activity that is done as a duty and not a pleasure is a chore, and while for a big family with a large garden and a small income, growing food may be essential, other families with smaller gardens should grow vegetables primarily for pleasure. Children enjoy helping to grow vegetables and can be encouraged to sow vegetable seeds in pots. When the seedlings are large enough, they can plant them out in the garden and later have fun harvesting the produce.

In a small garden, container-grown vegetables may be the only option. Fill a terra-cotta flowerpot with a potting mix that contains some soil, e.g. John Innes potting compost no. 2. Grow different vegetables in separate pots, and provide support when needed: plant runner beans in a large pot and then train them up a trellis tripod.

Another idea when garden space is limited is to grow vegetables in the mixed border. Lettuces, particularly the red-leaved variety "Red Salad Bowl", make a most attractive edging, and the feathery foliage of carrots is equally suitable for edging a border. Vegetables planted in a border need to be accessible for harvesting their leaves or fruit, so make sure you plant them where they can be reached and not behind a thorny rose or a delicate peony.

PROJECT	MAKING A RUNNER BEAN TEPEE

1 Mark out a circle 5ft (1.5m) in diameter and dig out a trench 4in (10cm) deep. Level the ground and lay out a water-permeable weed fabric membrane, pushing the extra material into the trench and covering it with soil.

2 Place some tall bamboo canes around the circle roughly 2ft (60cm) apart, leaving a wider gap for the tepee entrance. Push the bamboo canes in at an angle, at least 1ft (30cm) into the ground or until they are firm.

3 Tie the canes together in the middle with garden twine 6in (15cm) below the top of the poles. Plant a runner bean plant on the outside of each of the poles, and water in well.

4 Sow a circle of carrots around the outside of the runner beans, leaving the entrance to the tepee clear.

5 To protect the beans, tie rows of garden string around the circle of bamboos 2in (5cm), 4in (10cm), and 6in (15cm) up, leaving the entrance clear.

6 Ensure that the beans twine around the poles rather than dangling in midair. Add a couple of small paving stones to give dry access to the tepee during rain showers.

THE VEGETABLE GARDEN

If you want a separate vegetable garden, select a place that is sunny all day and where the soil is deep and fertile. Vegetables are usually grown in straight lines so it helps if the area is regular in shape. Allow room for the compost heap. Traditionally, vegetable gardens had several beds to allow for rotation of crops. If there is room for only a single bed, you will need to be careful about which crops you grow to avoid building up pest and disease problems.

BELOW *Plants for the kitchen can be both productive and decorative. Think also about* *"companion planting"—the use of certain other plants that help to ward off pests.*

FRUIT TREES

Unless you are lucky enough to have a very large garden, there is unlikely to be room for an orchard, but in even the smallest garden there may be space for a cordon fruit tree or two. Cordons have single stems with stubby side branches on which the fruit develop, and both apples and pears can be bought as cordons. They will need to be trained up wires on a wall or trellis, and will require annual pruning to keep them in shape. A single cordon fruit tree can produce up to 5lb (2.2kg) of fruit a year, so even a short row of them should provide the family with plenty of homegrown fruit.

PROJECT   **CIRCULAR HERB GARDEN**

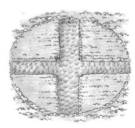

1 Locate the area for your herb circle and then fix a stake or peg in the center. Tie some string loosely to the stake or peg, and mark it at 2ft (75cm) from the peg. Walk around the peg keeping the string taut, and mark the radius with sand.

2 Dig the ground within the marked circle thoroughly to remove all existing weeds. Rake the soil roughly level and then mark out the center slab area and the crossing paths. Remove soil from these areas, then rake and firm the areas.

3 The paths and slab can be laid simply on a bed of sand or, for more stability, on a 3in (7.5cm) layer of stone and mortar with mortared joints.

4 Fork over the areas to be planted and then plant the four herb plants as shown in the diagram. Water in well after planting.

5 Rake a 6in (15cm) wide strip around the edge of the circle and then sow annual herbs in the strip. Cover the seeds with sifted soil and water gently.

6 Complete the garden by adding a pot planted with mint to the center slab.

A POND FOR WILDLIFE

A pond, however small, introduces a whole new range of wildlife into the garden, from dragonflies and water boatmen to newts, frogs, and toads. There is no need to bring in any of these animals—just create a water garden and they will arrive almost overnight.

Ponds naturally occur in hollows in the landscape where water collects and cannot escape, so if there is a low point already in your garden then this is probably the best site for a pond. Otherwise choose a site for your pond bearing in mind the criteria in the box below.

DESIGNING THE POND

An informal shape looks more natural, but if the pond is close to the house you may want a formal design to complement the shape of the house or terrace. Try to keep the shape simple, because complex shapes are difficult to construct and can look awkward. Make sure that there is a gradual slope into the water somewhere, so that different animals and birds can reach the water to drink in safety and frogs and toads can climb out.

Part of the pleasure of a wildlife pond is viewing the various inhabitants, so place some stones at the water's edge to allow the family safe and easy access; these stones will also allow birds to get to the water to drink.

PLANTING THE POND

Any pool of water eventually becomes colonized by plants but the first to arrive are algae. In the space of a few days they can turn a pool of clear water into a thick green "soup". The best method of controlling the algae is to plant the pond in early summer with a range of plants that will either compete with the algae for food or cover the pool surface with foliage and so deprive the algae of sunlight. A wildlife pond should be planted with native plants rather than exotics, as these are more attractive to native fauna.

There are several different categories of native plants. Oxygenating plants are essential as they live below the surface of the water and compete with the algae for food. They have simple roots and will establish more quickly if planted in water plant containers and placed on the base of the pool, rather than simply being dropped into the water. There are several to choose from and it is best to plant a selection.

LEFT *Pond plants are available from specialty suppliers. They require aquatic soil.*

WATCHPOINTS

🍃 Ponds need to be in sun for most of the day—most water plants prefer full sunlight and shady ponds attract relatively little wildlife.

🍃 Choose a site away from overhanging trees—in autumn the leaves fall into the pond and can cause problems.

🍃 Try to build your pond close to other vegetation—adjacent shrubs, hedges, and beds and borders will give cover to small mammals visiting the pond.

🍃 Choose a site sheltered from strong winds.

🍃 Your pond must be sufficiently deep that the water will not freeze solid in winter or overheat in summer—have at least part of the pond a minimum of 3ft (90cm) deep.

Floating aquatic plants float on the surface of the pond and reduce the amount of sunlight reaching the water. This deprives the algae of light and thereby helps to restrict their growth. Check that the floating plants you select are hardy and then place them on the surface of the pond in late spring and leave to grow.

PROJECT | MAKING A WILDLIFE POND USING A LINER

1 Mark out the shape of the pond on the ground, including any areas that are to be used for bog plants.

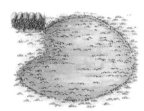

2 Remove the surface vegetation. If this is grass, lift sod carefully so that it can be used elsewhere in the garden.

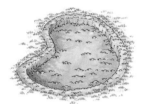

3 Carefully remove the topsoil and store for reuse later.

4 Put in a datum peg to establish the level of the finished pond, then add further pegs around the proposed edge. Use a spirit level and board to ensure that all the pegs are level.

5 Dig out the subsoil to create the pond, allowing for slopes and shelves as planned.

6 Cover the base, sides, and shelves with sand or fiber matting to protect the liner from being punctured by stones in the subsoil.

7 Lay the liner over the hole, pulling it taut and placing stones on the edge to hold in position. Make sure that the overlap is evenly distributed.

8 Gradually fill the liner with water so that it stretches to fit the shape of the hole.

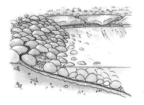

9 Cover the edges of the pond with gravel or stones for the sloping beach, paving for the viewing area, and soil for planting areas.

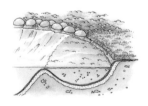

10 Use stored sod to replace any damaged grass areas, and then return topsoil to planted areas.

11 Top up water level and add containers of oxygenating, aquatic, and marginal plants; place floating plants on the surface of the pond.

12 Plant any planting areas around the pond.

THE PLANT DIRECTORY

This section contains 44 pages of plant entries to help you to select the best plants to grow in your family garden. Apart from the last eight pages, which specify plants to avoid, all the plants selected are those that could be included in your family garden. Whether you are looking for plants for children to grow themselves, a range of easy-to-grow, problem-free plants for the rest of the garden, or plants to eat, they can all be found in the following pages.

LEFT Nepeta x faasseni *(catmint) is planted here to soften the edge of a brick garden path.*

HOW TO USE THIS DIRECTORY

*T*he Plant Directory lists all the plants that are featured in this book, together with a selection of other plants that are suitable for use in a family garden. It is not intended to be exhaustive, and experienced gardeners will have their own favorites. However, this listing has been made with the specific requirements of a family garden in mind, and will guide the beginner to a range of attractive and readily available plants, shrubs, and trees with which to create a beautiful garden. Complete information on planting and maintaining the plants is given for each entry.

The Plant Directory is divided into different categories that group like plants together. The categories are annuals and biennials *(page 64)*, bulbs and corms *(page 70)*, herbaceous perennials *(page 72)*, shrubs *(page 82)*, roses *(page 86)*, conifers *(page 87)*, climbers *(page 88)*, trees *(page 90)*, vegetables and fruit *(page 92)*, and herbs *(page 96)*. At the end of the directory there is a listing of plants that are inappropriate for use in a family garden for various reasons. These are grouped together as plants that can cause skin rashes *(page 100)*, plants with thorns and prickles *(page 102)*, and poisonous plants *(page 104)*. The symbols panel accompanying each entry gives essential information on such things as growing conditions, light preference, and seasons of interest.

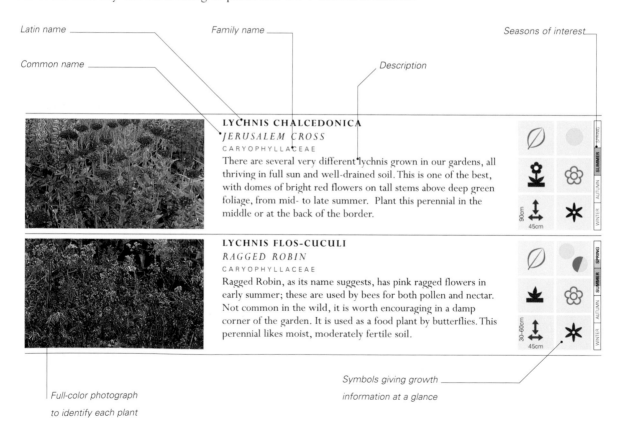

Latin name

Common name

Family name

Description

Seasons of interest

LYCHNIS CHALCEDONICA
JERUSALEM CROSS
CARYOPHYLLACEAE
There are several very different lychnis grown in our gardens, all thriving in full sun and well-drained soil. This is one of the best, with domes of bright red flowers on tall stems above deep green foliage, from mid- to late summer. Plant this perennial in the middle or at the back of the border.

LYCHNIS FLOS-CUCULI
RAGGED ROBIN
CARYOPHYLLACEAE
Ragged Robin, as its name suggests, has pink ragged flowers in early summer; these are used by bees for both pollen and nectar. Not common in the wild, it is worth encouraging in a damp corner of the garden. It is used as a food plant by butterflies. This perennial likes moist, moderately fertile soil.

Full-color photograph
to identify each plant

Symbols giving growth
information at a glance

KEY TO THE SYMBOLS

 EASY TO GROW

These are tolerant plants that require no special care or conditions in order to flourish.

 MODERATE TO GROW

These are plants that require some special care, such as protection from frost.

DIFFICULT TO GROW

These are plants that require a great deal of specialized care, and offer a challenge for the more experienced gardener.

EVERGREEN

SEMIEVERGREEN

DECIDUOUS

Deciduous plants lose all their leaves in autumn (sometimes in summer), while evergreen plants keep their foliage all year. Plants described as semievergreen may keep some or all of their foliage through the winter in sheltered gardens or if the weather is mild.

 **FEATURE LEAVES**

FEATURE SCENT

FEATURE FLOWER

FEATURE FRUIT

These symbols indicate the main feature of interest for each plant in the directory, although this is not necessarily the plant's only attractive asset. Some plants are given more than one symbol. This information will help you to choose plants that have complementary features, or plants that will perform a specific function in your garden.

 RAPID GROWTH

MODERATE GROWTH

SLOW GROWTH

Speed of growth is a highly subjective category, and will vary according to local conditions. Rapid growth indicates plants that reach their full extent in a single season, or plants that make substantial progress toward filling the space allowed for them in a single season. Slow growth indicates plants that take several seasons to reach their ultimate size. Moderate growth refers to rates of progress between these two extremes.

SEASON OF INTEREST

The period of the year when a plant is likely to be most attractive is also indicated (those plants that have something to offer all year round are marked accordingly). This will help you in creating a planting plan for each season.

HARDINESS ZONES

An indication of the frost-hardiness of each plant is given (a zone map can be found on page 112). In the case of annuals and tender perennials, you should check with your supplier to make sure you can offer the plant the right growing conditions.

 **HEIGHT AND SPREAD**

The size of plants will vary according to the growing conditions in your garden, so these measurements are a rough guide only. The measurements refer to the size of plants and trees when mature, although there are specific circumstances where the ultimate size is never reached.

 FULL SUN

PARTIAL SUN

SHADE

An indication of light preference is given to show each plant's optimum growing situation. Here again, this is only a rough guide, as some plants that prefer sun may also be reasonably tolerant of shade.

ANNUALS AND BIENNIALS

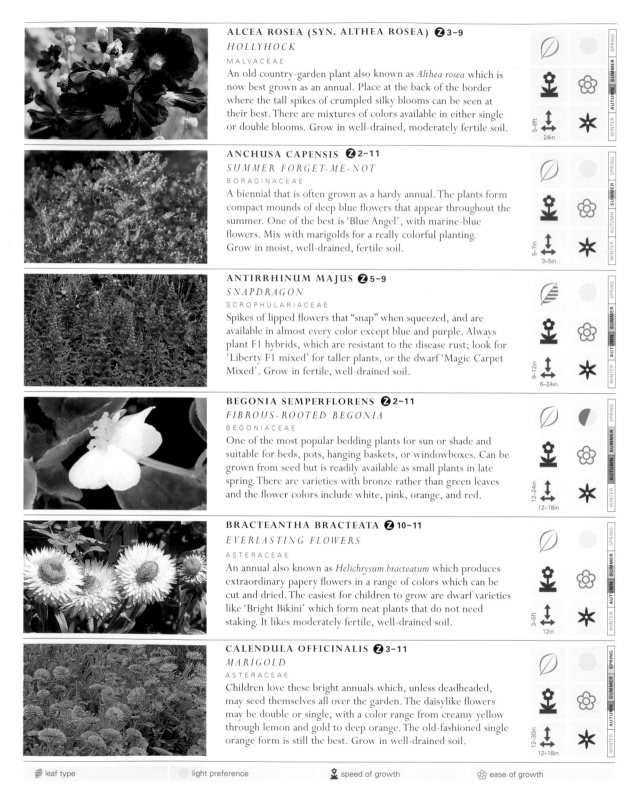

ALCEA ROSEA (SYN. ALTHEA ROSEA) Ⓩ 3–9
HOLLYHOCK

MALVACEAE

An old country-garden plant also known as *Althea rosea* which is now best grown as an annual. Place at the back of the border where the tall spikes of crumpled silky blooms can be seen at their best. There are mixtures of colors available in either single or double blooms. Grow in well-drained, moderately fertile soil.

5–8ft ↕ 24in

ANCHUSA CAPENSIS Ⓩ 2–11
SUMMER FORGET-ME-NOT

BORAGINACEAE

A biennial that is often grown as a hardy annual. The plants form compact mounds of deep blue flowers that appear throughout the summer. One of the best is 'Blue Angel', with marine-blue flowers. Mix with marigolds for a really colorful planting. Grow in moist, well-drained, fertile soil.

5–7in ↕ 3–5in

ANTIRRHINUM MAJUS Ⓩ 5–9
SNAPDRAGON

SCROPHULARIACEAE

Spikes of lipped flowers that "snap" when squeezed, and are available in almost every color except blue and purple. Always plant F1 hybrids, which are resistant to the disease rust; look for 'Liberty F1 mixed' for taller plants, or the dwarf 'Magic Carpet Mixed'. Grow in fertile, well-drained soil.

9–12in ↕ 6–24in

BEGONIA SEMPERFLORENS Ⓩ 2–11
FIBROUS-ROOTED BEGONIA

BEGONIACEAE

One of the most popular bedding plants for sun or shade and suitable for beds, pots, hanging baskets, or windowboxes. Can be grown from seed but is readily available as small plants in late spring. There are varieties with bronze rather than green leaves and the flower colors include white, pink, orange, and red.

12–24in ↕ 12–18in

BRACTEANTHA BRACTEATA Ⓩ 10–11
EVERLASTING FLOWERS

ASTERACEAE

An annual also known as *Helichrysum bracteatum* which produces extraordinary papery flowers in a range of colors which can be cut and dried. The easiest for children to grow are dwarf varieties like 'Bright Bikini' which form neat plants that do not need staking. It likes moderately fertile, well-drained soil.

3–5ft ↕ 12in

CALENDULA OFFICINALIS Ⓩ 3–11
MARIGOLD

ASTERACEAE

Children love these bright annuals which, unless deadheaded, may seed themselves all over the garden. The daisylike flowers may be double or single, with a color range from creamy yellow through lemon and gold to deep orange. The old-fashioned single orange form is still the best. Grow in well-drained soil.

12–30in ↕ 12–18in

≡ leaf type   ○ light preference   ⚘ speed of growth   ⚙ ease of growth

CENTAUREA CYANUS ❷ 2–11
CORNFLOWER
ASTERACEAE
Cornflower has dark blue, thistlelike flowers on wiry stems.
There are a range of cultivated varieties including white, pink,
and maroon flowers. The best variety for children to grow is the
dwarf blue 'Blue Baby', which will stay neat and tidy whatever
the weather. This annual likes well-drained soil.

CLARKIA AMOENA (SYN. GODETIA GRANDIFLORA)
GODETIA   ❷ 2–11
ONAGRACEAE
Another easy annual for children to grow, with large papery
flowers in July and August. Look for the smaller varieties like
'Salmon Princess' with pink flowers or 'Dwarf Satin' with
assorted colors, as these will not need staking. They are good for
any soil, including poor soils.

CLARKIA UNGUICULATA (SYN. CLARKIA ELEGANS)
ONAGRACEAE   ❷ 2–11
A vigorous annual that bears spikes of ruffle-edged flowers that
look like miniature hollyhocks. The flowers can be red, pink, or
mauve, and occasionally white. Easy to grow as long as they are
sown where they are to flower as they dislike being moved. It
likes soil that is moderately fertile, well drained, but moist and,
if possible, slightly acid.

COSMOS BIPINNATUS ❷ 3–10
COSMOS
ASTERACEAE
A lovely annual for dry soils and full sun, with ferny leaves and
flowers like a single dahlia. Older varieties have white or pink
flowers, but there are newer cultivars with red, striped, and even
chocolate-colored flowers. Plant in a group or among taller
plants. Prefers well-drained, sandy soil.

DIANTHUS BARBATUS ❷ 3–9
SWEET WILLIAM
CARYOPHYLLACEAE
An annual or biennial with a wonderful scent that children love.
The flat heads of massed flowers are available in white, pink, and
red, and in a range of types from tall varieties grown as biennials
to the dwarf 'Wee Willie', which is only 6in (15cm) high and
grown as an annual. It likes any well-drained soil.

ERIGERON 'KARVINSKIANUS' ❷ 5–7
SPANISH DAISY
ASTERACEAE
A spreading plant that is covered with pink-backed white daisies
that turn pink and then almost purple as they age. They flower all
summer long and are best planted as small plants and allowed
plenty of room. An excellent choice for children's windowboxes
and containers. It likes any well-drained soil.

⬍ height and spread   ✳ feature of interest   ▮▮▮ season of interest   *ANNUALS AND BIENNIALS* **A – E**

ANNUALS AND BIENNIALS

ESCHSCHOLZIA CALIFORNICA ⓩ 2–11
CALIFORNIAN POPPY
PAPAVERACEAE

One of the easiest of all plants to grow; just sprinkle the seed on bare ground in autumn or spring and watch the soft, blue-gray, divided leaves appear, followed by silky flowers in a range of colors from the original yellow and orange to the newer whites, pinks, reds, and purples. It likes poor, well-drained soil.

FELICIA BERGERIANA ⓩ 7–8
KINGFISHER DAISY
ASTERACEAE

This pretty, low-growing plant has turquoise-blue daisy flowers with yellow centers on stems less than 6in (15cm) long. The taller growing species is *Felicia amelloides* which has a variegated form that is most attractive. Plant in borders or containers in sandy soil and in full sun.

HELIANTHUS ANNUUS ⓩ 2–11
SUNFLOWER
ASTERACEAE

One of the best plants for children to grow, whether in their garden or in a pot. The race to grow the tallest, or largest, sunflower is an excellent introduction for children into the pleasure of growing plants. There are dwarf varieties for general planting. Grow in fertile, moist, but well-drained soil.

IBERIS UMBELLATA ⓩ 2–11
CANDYTUFT
BRASSICACEAE

One of the easiest plants for even the smallest member of the family to grow. It tolerates poor soil and pollution and produces masses of fragrant white or pink flowers. One of the best varieties for children is 'Fairy Mixed', with a mixture of pale pinks and white.

IMPATIENS WALLERIANA ⓩ 2–9
BUSY LIZZIE
BALSAMINACEAE

A very popular annual for shady gardens, there is now a wide range of white-, pink-, red-, or orange-flowered busy Lizzies with green, brown, or variegated leaves—enough choice for everyone. They are happy in the sun as long as they get plenty of water. Good for containers and hanging baskets. Grow in most soils.

LAVATERA TRIMESTRIS ⓩ 2–11
ANNUAL MALLOW
MALVACEAE

An easy-to-grow annual that forms a bushy plant with attractive lobed leaves and large, trumpet-shaped, silky-petaled flowers throughout summer. Beautiful varieties include 'Mont Blanc' with white flowers, 'Silver Cup' (pale pink), and 'Ruby Regis' (rosy red). It likes light, fertile, well-drained soil.

⬚ leaf type   ● light preference   ⚘ speed of growth   ❀ ease of growth

LIMNANTHES DOUGLASII ❂ 2–11

POACHED EGG PLANT

LIMANTHACEAE

The poached egg plant, as its name suggests, has flowers with white edges and golden yellow centers. Very easy to grow, there is the added bonus of pretty ferny leaves and a delicate scent. It tends to spread seed all over the garden, so be warned! Grow in fertile, moist, but well-drained soil.

6in / 6in

LOBELIA ERINUS ❂ 2–11

LOBELIA

CAMPANULACEAE

Used for generations as a bedding plant with alyssum and salvias, the blue-flowered lobelia is still as popular as ever. Use the dwarf forms like 'Crystal Palace' as edging, and the trailing ones like 'Sapphire' to cascade over the edges of hanging baskets. Water well in dry weather and grow in slightly moist soil.

4–9in / 4–6in

LOBULARIA MARITIMA ❂ 2–9

SWEET ALYSSUM

BRASSICACEAE

This annual, also known as *Alyssum maritimum*, has been used for years as part of colorful bedding plans. The leaves are covered with scented white flowers through summer. Easy to grow in all but very fertile soils, there are now newer varieties with lilac and purple flowers.

2–12in / 8–12in

LUNARIA ANNUA ❂ 5–9

HONESTY

BRASSICACEAE

Produces loose clusters of scented purple or white flowers then disklike pods that can be carefully split to unfold the silvery plate in the middle. This biennial is an important food plant for caterpillars. Sow seeds at the back of a border in moist but well-drained soil and allow plants to self-seed.

36in / 12in

MATTHIOLA BICORNIS ❂ 2–11

NIGHT-SCENTED STOCK

BRASSICACEAE

This annual may be a mistake to give to children, as they may insist on staying up to smell the purple flowers which open to release their rich fragrance as the sun sets. It is so easy to grow that it is a must for the whole family. Grow in moist, but well-drained, moderately fertile soil.

12–14in / 9in

MYOSOTIS ALPESTRIS ❂ 4–8

FORGET-ME-NOT

BORAGINACEAE

Forget-me-nots growing among tulips are a must for spring. There are now pink and white varieties, but the traditional blue is still the best, particularly the new dwarf 'Blue Ball'. These perennials, grown as biennials, freely self-seed and will appear year after year. Grow in moist, but well-drained soil.

8in / 6in

↕ height and spread   ✳ feature of interest   ▭▭▭ season of interest   *ANNUALS AND BIENNIALS* **E – M**

ANNUALS AND BIENNIALS

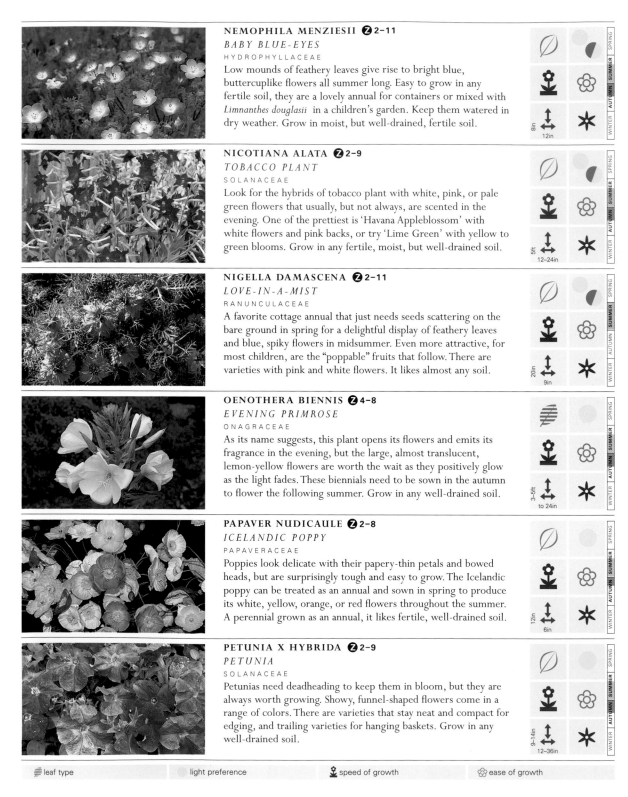

NEMOPHILA MENZIESII ❷ 2–11
BABY BLUE-EYES
HYDROPHYLLACEAE

Low mounds of feathery leaves give rise to bright blue, buttercuplike flowers all summer long. Easy to grow in any fertile soil, they are a lovely annual for containers or mixed with *Limnanthes douglasii* in a children's garden. Keep them watered in dry weather. Grow in moist, but well-drained, fertile soil.

NICOTIANA ALATA ❷ 2–9
TOBACCO PLANT
SOLANACEAE

Look for the hybrids of tobacco plant with white, pink, or pale green flowers that usually, but not always, are scented in the evening. One of the prettiest is 'Havana Appleblossom' with white flowers and pink backs, or try 'Lime Green' with yellow to green blooms. Grow in any fertile, moist, but well-drained soil.

NIGELLA DAMASCENA ❷ 2–11
LOVE-IN-A-MIST
RANUNCULACEAE

A favorite cottage annual that just needs seeds scattering on the bare ground in spring for a delightful display of feathery leaves and blue, spiky flowers in midsummer. Even more attractive, for most children, are the "poppable" fruits that follow. There are varieties with pink and white flowers. It likes almost any soil.

OENOTHERA BIENNIS ❷ 4–8
EVENING PRIMROSE
ONAGRACEAE

As its name suggests, this plant opens its flowers and emits its fragrance in the evening, but the large, almost translucent, lemon-yellow flowers are worth the wait as they positively glow as the light fades. These biennials need to be sown in the autumn to flower the following summer. Grow in any well-drained soil.

PAPAVER NUDICAULE ❷ 2–8
ICELANDIC POPPY
PAPAVERACEAE

Poppies look delicate with their papery-thin petals and bowed heads, but are surprisingly tough and easy to grow. The Icelandic poppy can be treated as an annual and sown in spring to produce its white, yellow, orange, or red flowers throughout the summer. A perennial grown as an annual, it likes fertile, well-drained soil.

PETUNIA X HYBRIDA ❷ 2–9
PETUNIA
SOLANACEAE

Petunias need deadheading to keep them in bloom, but they are always worth growing. Showy, funnel-shaped flowers come in a range of colors. There are varieties that stay neat and compact for edging, and trailing varieties for hanging baskets. Grow in any well-drained soil.

leaf type　　light preference　　speed of growth　　ease of growth

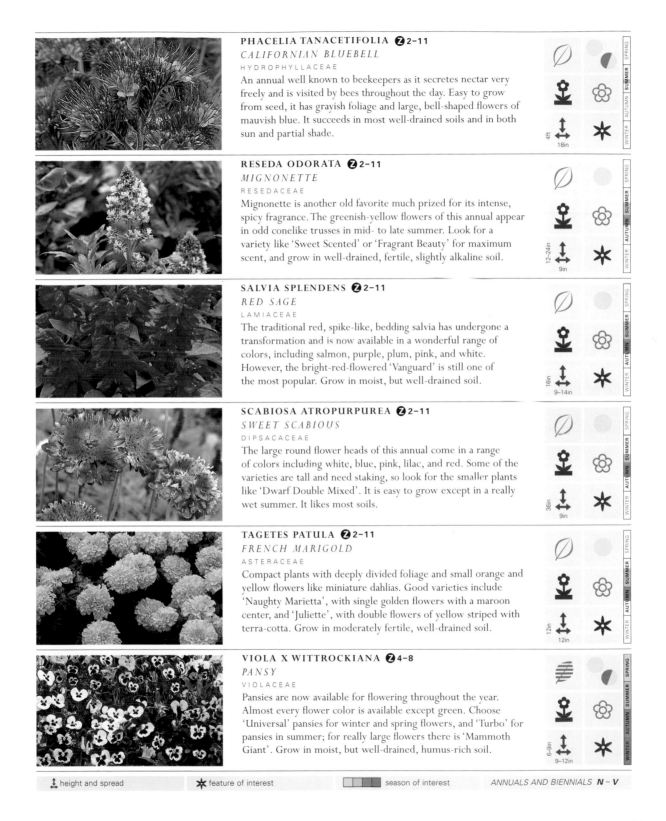

PHACELIA TANACETIFOLIA Ⓩ 2–11

CALIFORNIAN BLUEBELL

HYDROPHYLLACEAE

An annual well known to beekeepers as it secretes nectar very freely and is visited by bees throughout the day. Easy to grow from seed, it has grayish foliage and large, bell-shaped flowers of mauvish blue. It succeeds in most well-drained soils and in both sun and partial shade.

4ft / 18in

RESEDA ODORATA Ⓩ 2–11

MIGNONETTE

RESEDACEAE

Mignonette is another old favorite much prized for its intense, spicy fragrance. The greenish-yellow flowers of this annual appear in odd conelike trusses in mid- to late summer. Look for a variety like 'Sweet Scented' or 'Fragrant Beauty' for maximum scent, and grow in well-drained, fertile, slightly alkaline soil.

12–24in / 9in

SALVIA SPLENDENS Ⓩ 2–11

RED SAGE

LAMIACEAE

The traditional red, spike-like, bedding salvia has undergone a transformation and is now available in a wonderful range of colors, including salmon, purple, plum, pink, and white. However, the bright-red-flowered 'Vanguard' is still one of the most popular. Grow in moist, but well-drained soil.

16in / 9–14in

SCABIOSA ATROPURPUREA Ⓩ 2–11

SWEET SCABIOUS

DIPSACACEAE

The large round flower heads of this annual come in a range of colors including white, blue, pink, lilac, and red. Some of the varieties are tall and need staking, so look for the smaller plants like 'Dwarf Double Mixed'. It is easy to grow except in a really wet summer. It likes most soils.

36in / 9in

TAGETES PATULA Ⓩ 2–11

FRENCH MARIGOLD

ASTERACEAE

Compact plants with deeply divided foliage and small orange and yellow flowers like miniature dahlias. Good varieties include 'Naughty Marietta', with single golden flowers with a maroon center, and 'Juliette', with double flowers of yellow striped with terra-cotta. Grow in moderately fertile, well-drained soil.

12in / 12in

VIOLA X WITTROCKIANA Ⓩ 4–8

PANSY

VIOLACEAE

Pansies are now available for flowering throughout the year. Almost every flower color is available except green. Choose 'Universal' pansies for winter and spring flowers, and 'Turbo' for pansies in summer; for really large flowers there is 'Mammoth Giant'. Grow in moist, but well-drained, humus-rich soil.

6–9in / 9–12in

↕ height and spread   ✳ feature of interest   ▭ season of interest   *ANNUALS AND BIENNIALS **N – V***

BULBS

CROCUS X LUTEUS ❷ 3–8
CROCUS
IRIDACEAE

There are lots of different crocus species to grow, including those that flower in the autumn as well as the better-known late winter and early spring flowers. This is the large Dutch crocus, with yellow, white, or purple flowers in early spring, which is ideally suited to planting in grass. Grow in any well-drained soil.

3–4in / 3–4in

ERANTHIS HYEMALIS ❷ 4–9
WINTER ACONITE
RANUNCULACEAE

Winter aconites, together with snowdrops, are the earliest of the bulbs to flower; their glossy yellow flowers can appear in January or early February. Plant in the grass, or under trees and shrubs in fertile, humus-rich soil, to form a golden carpet, or, in a small garden, plant a small patch by the back door.

2–3in / 3in

GALANTHUS NIVALIS ❷ 3–9
SNOWDROP
AMARYLLIDACEAE

Snowdrops are the popular heralds of spring, with their nodding white and green flowers and dark green leaves. There are several different species and cultivars, with double flowers such as 'Flore Pleno'. Dried-out bulbs are not successful, so plant as soon as you get them. Grow in moist, but well-drained soil.

6in / 6in

HYACINTHOIDES NON-SCRIPTA ❷ 4–9
BLUEBELL
HYACINTHACEAE

Not a perennial for the small garden as you really need an area of woodland to grow bluebells successfully, but even a small grove of birch trees can be transformed with a carpet of bluebells in the spring. Plant in autumn as soon as possible after purchase. It likes moderately fertile, moist, but well-drained soil.

8–16in / 3in

HYACINTHUS ORIENTALIS ❷ 5–9
HYACINTH
HYACINTHACEAE

Hyacinths produce large trusses of scented flowers in spring, and are ideal for planting in containers or borders for a bright patch of color. The color range includes the traditional blue, pink, and white flowers, but also plum, apricot, and pale yellow. Grow in well-drained, moderately fertile soil.

8–12in / 6–8in

IRIS RETICULATA ❷ 5–8
DWARF IRIS
IRIDACEAE

There are dozens of different irises we can use in our gardens, but this is one of the smallest, earliest, and prettiest, with thin gray-green leaves and deep purple, sweetly scented flowers in early spring. Grow at the front of a bed or in pots near the house in moderately fertile, well-drained soil.

4–6in / 3–4in

≣ leaf type   ● light preference   🌷 speed of growth   ❀ ease of growth

LILIUM REGALE ❷4-7
REGAL LILY
LILIACEAE

If you grow just one lily it should be this one, with tall stems of large, white, trumpetlike flowers with pink stripes on the back of the petals, a yellow throat, and a wonderfully rich scent. The easiest way to grow lilies is in pots using organically rich compost, or well-drained, fertile soil.

2–6ft
10–16in

MUSCARI ARMENIACUM ❷4-8
GRAPE HYACINTH
HYACINTHACEAE

The flowers, which appear in spring, resemble miniature blue hyacinths and look wonderful planted with pink, white, or yellow tulips at the front of a border. Very easy to grow, it can also be used as ground cover under shrubs and will spread quite happily if left to itself. It likes moist, but well-drained soil.

to 8in
3–6in

NARCISSUS POETICUS ❷4-9
POET'S EYE NARCISSUS
AMARYLLIDACEAE

This narcissus has white petals and a small, frilled, red-edged cup. Very sweetly scented, it is almost the last of the narcissus to flower, and for that reason may be a problem grown in grass, as the grass will need cutting before the leaves have died down. It is best grown in borders or containers. Grow in any soil.

8–20in
to 6in

NARCISSUS PSEUDONARCISSUS ❷4-9
DAFFODIL
AMARYLLIDACEAE

This is a popular flower in British gardens, and a familiar sight planted in grass in the spring. Use the simpler, yellow-flowered varieties for planting in grass areas and keep the doubles, multicolors and frilly petaled cultivars to grow in beds, borders, and containers. Grow in any soil.

6–14in
4–6in

SCILLA SIBERICA ❷5-8
SCILLA
HYACINTHACEAE

Looking like small bluebells, scillas are very easy plants to grow. Once planted, they will happily spread through the garden, or as a carpet under trees and shrubs. Plant the bulbs immediately after purchase, as they are susceptible to decay when out of the soil. Grow in well-drained, moderately fertile soil.

4–8in
4–6in

TULIPA HYBRIDS ❷4-10
TULIP
LILIACEAE

Unsurpassed in their range of colors, tulips are also available in different heights and with different times of flowering, the earliest species being in flower with crocuses and the latest tulip hybrids flowering almost with the early roses. They are suitable for beds, borders, and containers. Grow in any soil.

6–26in
3–10in

↕ height and spread   ✳ feature of interest   ▭ season of interest   *BULBS* **C – T**

HERBACEOUS PERENNIALS

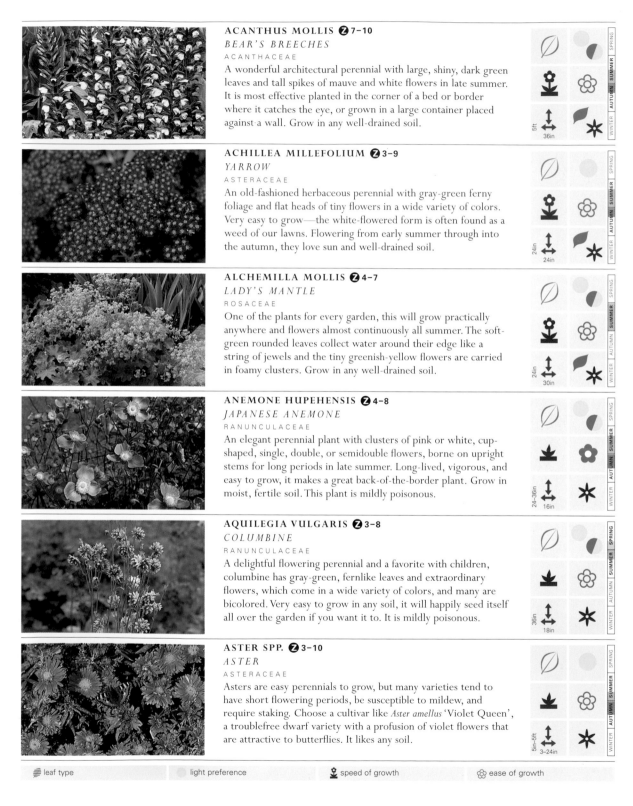

ACANTHUS MOLLIS ❷ 7–10
BEAR'S BREECHES
ACANTHACEAE

A wonderful architectural perennial with large, shiny, dark green leaves and tall spikes of mauve and white flowers in late summer. It is most effective planted in the corner of a bed or border where it catches the eye, or grown in a large container placed against a wall. Grow in any well-drained soil.

5ft / 36in

ACHILLEA MILLEFOLIUM ❷ 3–9
YARROW
ASTERACEAE

An old-fashioned herbaceous perennial with gray-green ferny foliage and flat heads of tiny flowers in a wide variety of colors. Very easy to grow—the white-flowered form is often found as a weed of our lawns. Flowering from early summer through into the autumn, they love sun and well-drained soil.

24in / 24in

ALCHEMILLA MOLLIS ❷ 4–7
LADY'S MANTLE
ROSACEAE

One of the plants for every garden, this will grow practically anywhere and flowers almost continuously all summer. The soft-green rounded leaves collect water around their edge like a string of jewels and the tiny greenish-yellow flowers are carried in foamy clusters. Grow in any well-drained soil.

24in / 30in

ANEMONE HUPEHENSIS ❷ 4–8
JAPANESE ANEMONE
RANUNCULACEAE

An elegant perennial plant with clusters of pink or white, cup-shaped, single, double, or semidouble flowers, borne on upright stems for long periods in late summer. Long-lived, vigorous, and easy to grow, it makes a great back-of-the-border plant. Grow in moist, fertile soil. This plant is mildly poisonous.

24–36in / 16in

AQUILEGIA VULGARIS ❷ 3–8
COLUMBINE
RANUNCULACEAE

A delightful flowering perennial and a favorite with children, columbine has gray-green, fernlike leaves and extraordinary flowers, which come in a wide variety of colors, and many are bicolored. Very easy to grow in any soil, it will happily seed itself all over the garden if you want it to. It is mildly poisonous.

36in / 18in

ASTER SPP. ❷ 3–10
ASTER
ASTERACEAE

Asters are easy perennials to grow, but many varieties tend to have short flowering periods, be susceptible to mildew, and require staking. Choose a cultivar like *Aster amellus* 'Violet Queen', a troublefree dwarf variety with a profusion of violet flowers that are attractive to butterflies. It likes any soil.

5in–5ft / 3–24in

SPRING | SUMMER | AUTUMN | WINTER

≋ leaf type ● light preference ⚘ speed of growth ⚘ ease of growth

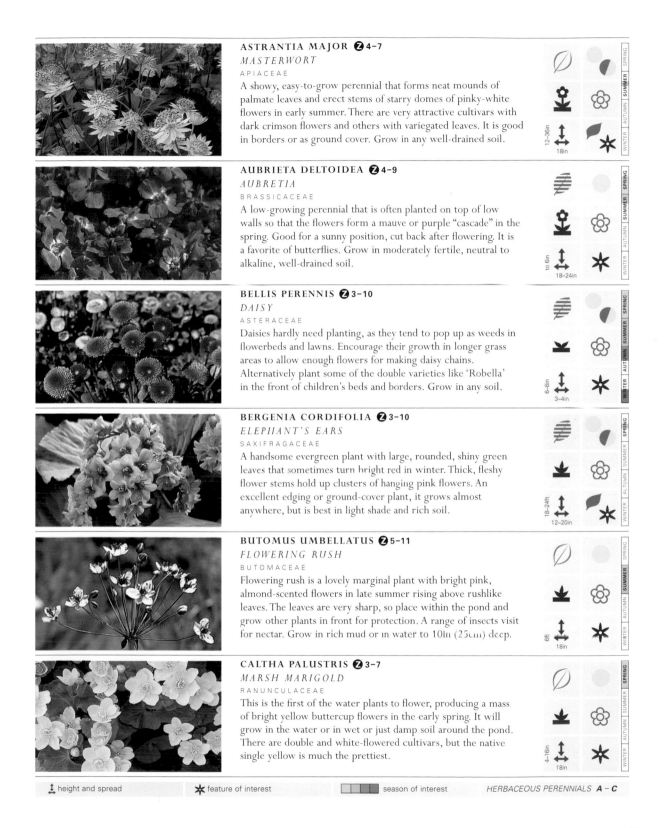

ASTRANTIA MAJOR ❷ 4–7
MASTERWORT
APIACEAE

A showy, easy-to-grow perennial that forms neat mounds of palmate leaves and erect stems of starry domes of pinky-white flowers in early summer. There are very attractive cultivars with dark crimson flowers and others with variegated leaves. It is good in borders or as ground cover. Grow in any well-drained soil.

12–36in
18in

AUBRIETA DELTOIDEA ❷ 4–9
AUBRETIA
BRASSICACEAE

A low-growing perennial that is often planted on top of low walls so that the flowers form a mauve or purple "cascade" in the spring. Good for a sunny position, cut back after flowering. It is a favorite of butterflies. Grow in moderately fertile, neutral to alkaline, well-drained soil.

to 6in
18–24in

BELLIS PERENNIS ❷ 3–10
DAISY
ASTERACEAE

Daisies hardly need planting, as they tend to pop up as weeds in flowerbeds and lawns. Encourage their growth in longer grass areas to allow enough flowers for making daisy chains. Alternatively plant some of the double varieties like 'Robella' in the front of children's beds and borders. Grow in any soil.

6–8in
3–4in

BERGENIA CORDIFOLIA ❷ 3–10
ELEPHANT'S EARS
SAXIFRAGACEAE

A handsome evergreen plant with large, rounded, shiny green leaves that sometimes turn bright red in winter. Thick, fleshy flower stems hold up clusters of hanging pink flowers. An excellent edging or ground-cover plant, it grows almost anywhere, but is best in light shade and rich soil.

18–24ft
12–20in

BUTOMUS UMBELLATUS ❷ 5–11
FLOWERING RUSH
BUTOMACEAE

Flowering rush is a lovely marginal plant with bright pink, almond-scented flowers in late summer rising above rushlike leaves. The leaves are very sharp, so place within the pond and grow other plants in front for protection. A range of insects visit for nectar. Grow in rich mud or in water to 10in (25cm) deep.

6ft
18in

CALTHA PALUSTRIS ❷ 3–7
MARSH MARIGOLD
RANUNCULACEAE

This is the first of the water plants to flower, producing a mass of bright yellow buttercup flowers in the early spring. It will grow in the water or in wet or just damp soil around the pond. There are double and white-flowered cultivars, but the native single yellow is much the prettiest.

4–16in
18in

SPRING | SUMMER | AUTUMN | WINTER

↕ height and spread   ✳ feature of interest   ▭▭▭ season of interest   *HERBACEOUS PERENNIALS* **A – C**

HERBACEOUS PERENNIALS

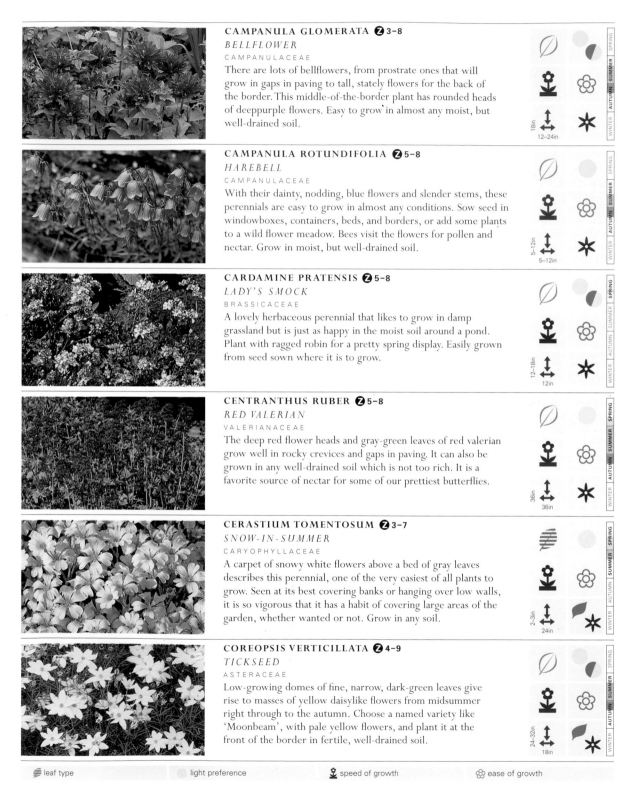

CAMPANULA GLOMERATA ❷ 3–8
BELLFLOWER
CAMPANULACEAE
There are lots of bellflowers, from prostrate ones that will
grow in gaps in paving to tall, stately flowers for the back of
the border. This middle-of-the-border plant has rounded heads
of deeppurple flowers. Easy to grow in almost any moist, but
well-drained soil.

18in
12–24in

CAMPANULA ROTUNDIFOLIA ❷ 5–8
HAREBELL
CAMPANULACEAE
With their dainty, nodding, blue flowers and slender stems, these
perennials are easy to grow in almost any conditions. Sow seed in
windowboxes, containers, beds, and borders, or add some plants
to a wild flower meadow. Bees visit the flowers for pollen and
nectar. Grow in moist, but well-drained soil.

5–12in
5–12in

CARDAMINE PRATENSIS ❷ 5–8
LADY'S SMOCK
BRASSICACEAE
A lovely herbaceous perennial that likes to grow in damp
grassland but is just as happy in the moist soil around a pond.
Plant with ragged robin for a pretty spring display. Easily grown
from seed sown where it is to grow.

12–18in
12in

CENTRANTHUS RUBER ❷ 5–8
RED VALERIAN
VALERIANACEAE
The deep red flower heads and gray-green leaves of red valerian
grow well in rocky crevices and gaps in paving. It can also be
grown in any well-drained soil which is not too rich. It is a
favorite source of nectar for some of our prettiest butterflies.

36in
36in

CERASTIUM TOMENTOSUM ❷ 3–7
SNOW-IN-SUMMER
CARYOPHYLLACEAE
A carpet of snowy white flowers above a bed of gray leaves
describes this perennial, one of the very easiest of all plants to
grow. Seen at its best covering banks or hanging over low walls,
it is so vigorous that it has a habit of covering large areas of the
garden, whether wanted or not. Grow in any soil.

2–3in
24in

COREOPSIS VERTICILLATA ❷ 4–9
TICKSEED
ASTERACEAE
Low-growing domes of fine, narrow, dark-green leaves give
rise to masses of yellow daisylike flowers from midsummer
right through to the autumn. Choose a named variety like
'Moonbeam', with pale yellow flowers, and plant it at the
front of the border in fertile, well-drained soil.

24–32in
18in

🗦 leaf type   light preference   ⚘ speed of growth   ✿ ease of growth

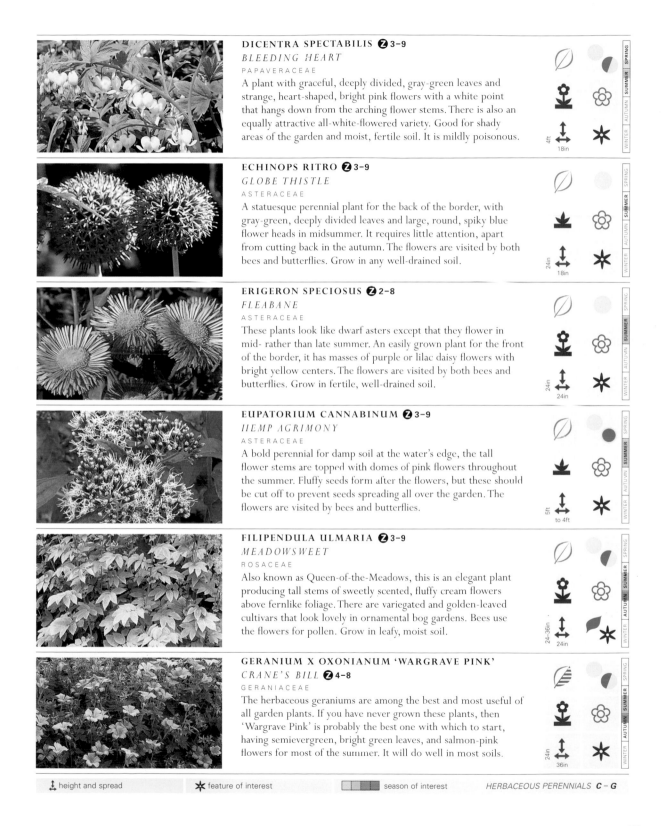

DICENTRA SPECTABILIS ⓩ 3–9

BLEEDING HEART

PAPAVERACEAE

A plant with graceful, deeply divided, gray-green leaves and strange, heart-shaped, bright pink flowers with a white point that hangs down from the arching flower stems. There is also an equally attractive all-white-flowered variety. Good for shady areas of the garden and moist, fertile soil. It is mildly poisonous.

4ft / 18in

ECHINOPS RITRO ⓩ 3–9

GLOBE THISTLE

ASTERACEAE

A statuesque perennial plant for the back of the border, with gray-green, deeply divided leaves and large, round, spiky blue flower heads in midsummer. It requires little attention, apart from cutting back in the autumn. The flowers are visited by both bees and butterflies. Grow in any well-drained soil.

24in / 18in

ERIGERON SPECIOSUS ⓩ 2–8

FLEABANE

ASTERACEAE

These plants look like dwarf asters except that they flower in mid- rather than late summer. An easily grown plant for the front of the border, it has masses of purple or lilac daisy flowers with bright yellow centers. The flowers are visited by both bees and butterflies. Grow in fertile, well-drained soil.

24in / 24in

EUPATORIUM CANNABINUM ⓩ 3–9

HEMP AGRIMONY

ASTERACEAE

A bold perennial for damp soil at the water's edge, the tall flower stems are topped with domes of pink flowers throughout the summer. Fluffy seeds form after the flowers, but these should be cut off to prevent seeds spreading all over the garden. The flowers are visited by bees and butterflies.

5ft / to 4ft

FILIPENDULA ULMARIA ⓩ 3–9

MEADOWSWEET

ROSACEAE

Also known as Queen-of-the-Meadows, this is an elegant plant producing tall stems of sweetly scented, fluffy cream flowers above fernlike foliage. There are variegated and golden-leaved cultivars that look lovely in ornamental bog gardens. Bees use the flowers for pollen. Grow in leafy, moist soil.

24–36in / 24in

GERANIUM X OXONIANUM 'WARGRAVE PINK'

CRANE'S BILL ⓩ 4–8

GERANIACEAE

The herbaceous geraniums are among the best and most useful of all garden plants. If you have never grown these plants, then 'Wargrave Pink' is probably the best one with which to start, having semievergreen, bright green leaves, and salmon-pink flowers for most of the summer. It will do well in most soils.

24in / 36in

↕ height and spread   ✴ feature of interest   ▭▭ season of interest   *HERBACEOUS PERENNIALS **C – G***

HERBACEOUS PERENNIALS

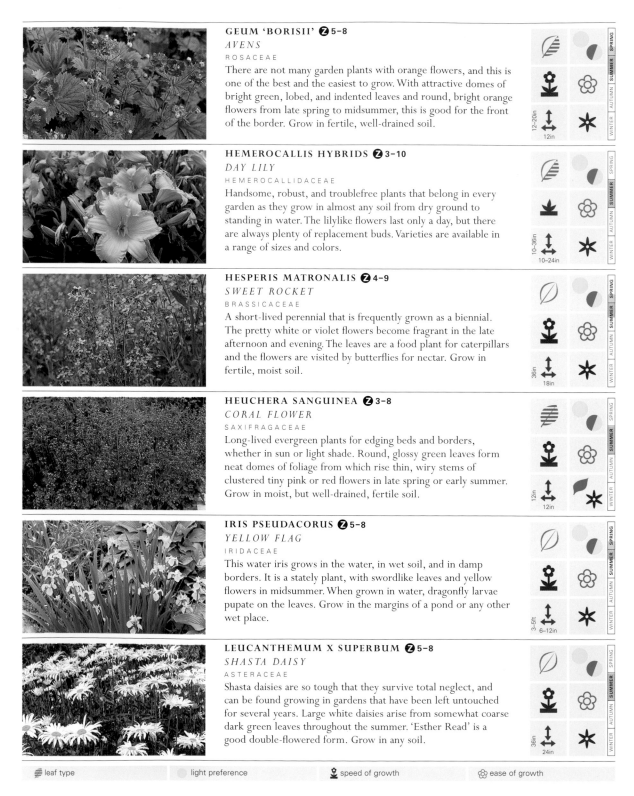

GEUM 'BORISII' ❷ 5–8
AVENS
ROSACEAE

There are not many garden plants with orange flowers, and this is one of the best and the easiest to grow. With attractive domes of bright green, lobed, and indented leaves and round, bright orange flowers from late spring to midsummer, this is good for the front of the border. Grow in fertile, well-drained soil.

12–20in
12in

HEMEROCALLIS HYBRIDS ❷ 3–10
DAY LILY
HEMEROCALLIDACEAE

Handsome, robust, and troublefree plants that belong in every garden as they grow in almost any soil from dry ground to standing in water. The lilylike flowers last only a day, but there are always plenty of replacement buds. Varieties are available in a range of sizes and colors.

10–36in
10–24in

HESPERIS MATRONALIS ❷ 4–9
SWEET ROCKET
BRASSICACEAE

A short-lived perennial that is frequently grown as a biennial. The pretty white or violet flowers become fragrant in the late afternoon and evening. The leaves are a food plant for caterpillars and the flowers are visited by butterflies for nectar. Grow in fertile, moist soil.

36in
18in

HEUCHERA SANGUINEA ❷ 3–8
CORAL FLOWER
SAXIFRAGACEAE

Long-lived evergreen plants for edging beds and borders, whether in sun or light shade. Round, glossy green leaves form neat domes of foliage from which rise thin, wiry stems of clustered tiny pink or red flowers in late spring or early summer. Grow in moist, but well-drained, fertile soil.

12in
12in

IRIS PSEUDACORUS ❷ 5–8
YELLOW FLAG
IRIDACEAE

This water iris grows in the water, in wet soil, and in damp borders. It is a stately plant, with swordlike leaves and yellow flowers in midsummer. When grown in water, dragonfly larvae pupate on the leaves. Grow in the margins of a pond or any other wet place.

3–5ft
6–12in

LEUCANTHEMUM X SUPERBUM ❷ 5–8
SHASTA DAISY
ASTERACEAE

Shasta daisies are so tough that they survive total neglect, and can be found growing in gardens that have been left untouched for several years. Large white daisies arise from somewhat coarse dark green leaves throughout the summer. 'Esther Read' is a good double-flowered form. Grow in any soil.

36in
24in

SPRING | SUMMER | AUTUMN | WINTER

≡ leaf type   ● light preference   ♣ speed of growth   ❀ ease of growth

LEUCANTHEMUM VULGARE ❷3-8

OX-EYE DAISY

ASTERACEAE

These large white and yellow perennials are one of the easiest wild flowers to grow, and they flower throughout the summer months. They can be planted in long grass as part of a wild flower meadow or as part of a planted bed or border. Easy to grow from seed sown where the plants are to flower. Grow in any soil.

12–36in / 24in

LINARIA VULGARIS ❷4-8

TOADFLAX

SCROPHULARIACEAE

Also called butter and eggs, the flowers of this plant resemble small yellow snapdragons and hold a fascination for small children. It can be grown from seed and is best grown in grass areas or the wild garden. An important nectar plant for many bees. Grow in moderately fertile, light, sandy soil.

12in / 12in

LIRIOPE MUSCARI ❷6-10

LILY TURF

CONVALLARIACEAE

A less frequently seen perennial with dark green, straplike, arching leaves and low spikes of purple flowers in late summer right through the autumn. Easy to grow in sun or shade, the foliage is evergreen and it makes a good edging plant or ground cover beneath shrubs. Grow in well-drained soil.

12in / 18in

LOTUS CORNICULATUS ❷5-8

BIRD'S FOOT TREFOIL

PAPILIONACEAE

A little herbaceous perennial that produces a cluster of bright yellow pea flowers, succeeded by black pods that look like a claw or "bird's foot". Easy to grow from seed, it is an important food plant for the larvae of several butterflies. It likes any well-drained soil.

8–12in / 12in

LYCHNIS CHALCEDONICA ❷4-8

JERUSALEM CROSS

CARYOPHYLLACEAE

There are several very different lychnis to grow in our gardens, all thriving in full sun and well-drained soil. This is one of the best, with domes of bright red flowers on tall stems above deep green foliage, from mid- to late summer. Plant this perennial in the middle or at the back of the border.

3–4ft / 12in

LYCHNIS FLOS-CUCULI ❷6-9

RAGGED ROBIN

CARYOPHYLLACEAE

Ragged Robin, as its name suggests, has pink ragged flowers in early summer; these are used by bees for both pollen and nectar. Not common in the wild, it is worth encouraging in a damp corner of the garden. It is used as a food plant by butterflies. This perennial likes moist, moderately fertile soil.

30in / 32in

⬍ height and spread   ✳ feature of interest   ▭ season of interest   *HERBACEOUS PERENNIALS* **G – L**

HERBACEOUS PERENNIALS

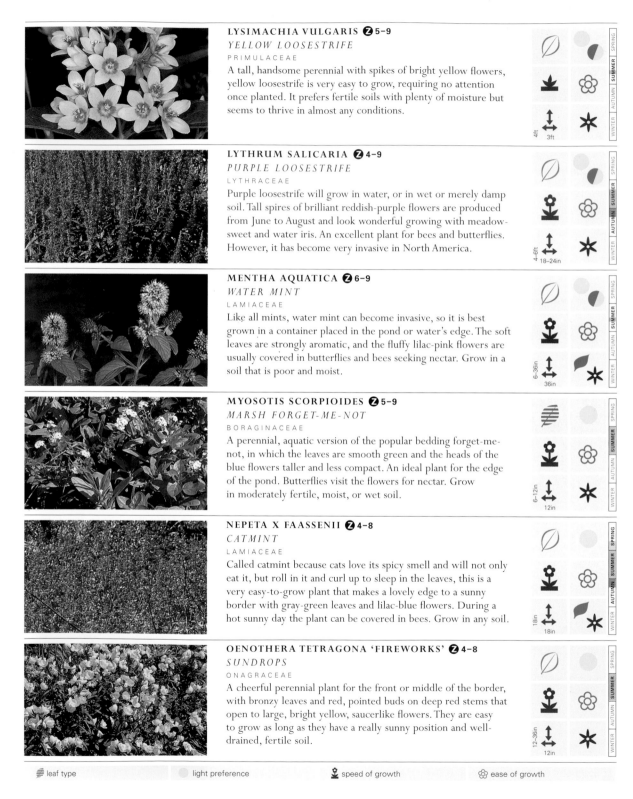

LYSIMACHIA VULGARIS **Z** 5–9
YELLOW LOOSESTRIFE
PRIMULACEAE

A tall, handsome perennial with spikes of bright yellow flowers, yellow loosestrife is very easy to grow, requiring no attention once planted. It prefers fertile soils with plenty of moisture but seems to thrive in almost any conditions.

LYTHRUM SALICARIA **Z** 4–9
PURPLE LOOSESTRIFE
LYTHRACEAE

Purple loosestrife will grow in water, or in wet or merely damp soil. Tall spires of brilliant reddish-purple flowers are produced from June to August and look wonderful growing with meadow-sweet and water iris. An excellent plant for bees and butterflies. However, it has become very invasive in North America.

MENTHA AQUATICA **Z** 6–9
WATER MINT
LAMIACEAE

Like all mints, water mint can become invasive, so it is best grown in a container placed in the pond or water's edge. The soft leaves are strongly aromatic, and the fluffy lilac-pink flowers are usually covered in butterflies and bees seeking nectar. Grow in a soil that is poor and moist.

MYOSOTIS SCORPIOIDES **Z** 5–9
MARSH FORGET-ME-NOT
BORAGINACEAE

A perennial, aquatic version of the popular bedding forget-me-not, in which the leaves are smooth green and the heads of the blue flowers taller and less compact. An ideal plant for the edge of the pond. Butterflies visit the flowers for nectar. Grow in moderately fertile, moist, or wet soil.

NEPETA X FAASSENII **Z** 4–8
CATMINT
LAMIACEAE

Called catmint because cats love its spicy smell and will not only eat it, but roll in it and curl up to sleep in the leaves, this is a very easy-to-grow plant that makes a lovely edge to a sunny border with gray-green leaves and lilac-blue flowers. During a hot sunny day the plant can be covered in bees. Grow in any soil.

OENOTHERA TETRAGONA 'FIREWORKS' **Z** 4–8
SUNDROPS
ONAGRACEAE

A cheerful perennial plant for the front or middle of the border, with bronzy leaves and red, pointed buds on deep red stems that open to large, bright yellow, saucerlike flowers. They are easy to grow as long as they have a really sunny position and well-drained, fertile soil.

≣ leaf type   ● light preference   ⚑ speed of growth   ✿ ease of growth

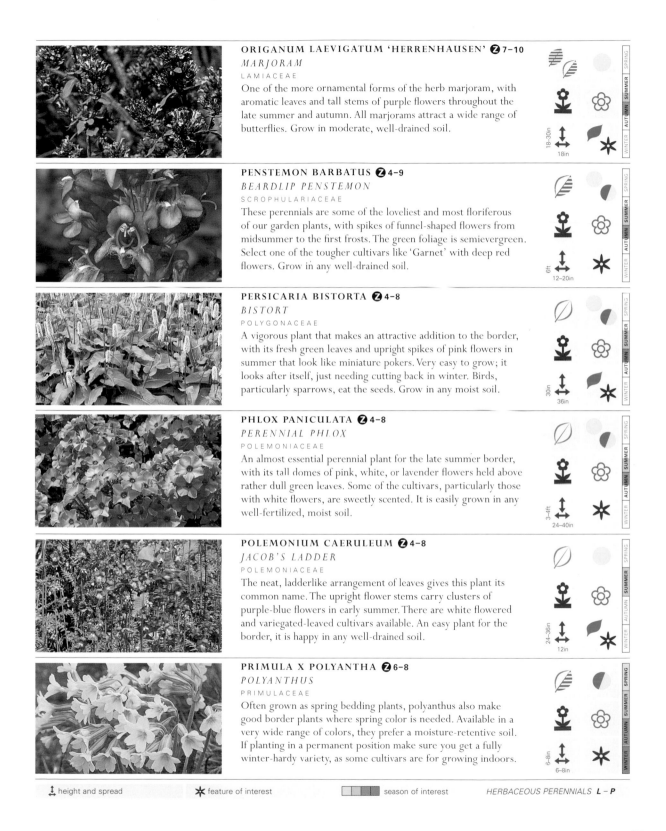

ORIGANUM LAEVIGATUM 'HERRENHAUSEN' **Z** 7–10
MARJORAM
LAMIACEAE
One of the more ornamental forms of the herb marjoram, with aromatic leaves and tall stems of purple flowers throughout the late summer and autumn. All marjorams attract a wide range of butterflies. Grow in moderate, well-drained soil.

18–30in
18in

PENSTEMON BARBATUS **Z** 4–9
BEARDLIP PENSTEMON
SCROPHULARIACEAE
These perennials are some of the loveliest and most floriferous of our garden plants, with spikes of funnel-shaped flowers from midsummer to the first frosts. The green foliage is semievergreen. Select one of the tougher cultivars like 'Garnet' with deep red flowers. Grow in any well-drained soil.

6ft
12–20in

PERSICARIA BISTORTA **Z** 4–8
BISTORT
POLYGONACEAE
A vigorous plant that makes an attractive addition to the border, with its fresh green leaves and upright spikes of pink flowers in summer that look like miniature pokers. Very easy to grow; it looks after itself, just needing cutting back in winter. Birds, particularly sparrows, eat the seeds. Grow in any moist soil.

30in
36in

PHLOX PANICULATA **Z** 4–8
PERENNIAL PHLOX
POLEMONIACEAE
An almost essential perennial plant for the late summer border, with its tall domes of pink, white, or lavender flowers held above rather dull green leaves. Some of the cultivars, particularly those with white flowers, are sweetly scented. It is easily grown in any well-fertilized, moist soil.

3–4ft
24–40in

POLEMONIUM CAERULEUM **Z** 4–8
JACOB'S LADDER
POLEMONIACEAE
The neat, ladderlike arrangement of leaves gives this plant its common name. The upright flower stems carry clusters of purple-blue flowers in early summer. There are white flowered and variegated-leaved cultivars available. An easy plant for the border, it is happy in any well-drained soil.

24–36in
12in

PRIMULA X POLYANTHA **Z** 6–8
POLYANTHUS
PRIMULACEAE
Often grown as spring bedding plants, polyanthus also make good border plants where spring color is needed. Available in a very wide range of colors, they prefer a moisture-retentive soil. If planting in a permanent position make sure you get a fully winter-hardy variety, as some cultivars are for growing indoors.

6–8in
6–8in

↕ height and spread   ✱ feature of interest   ▭▭▭ season of interest   *HERBACEOUS PERENNIALS* **L – P**

HERBACEOUS PERENNIALS

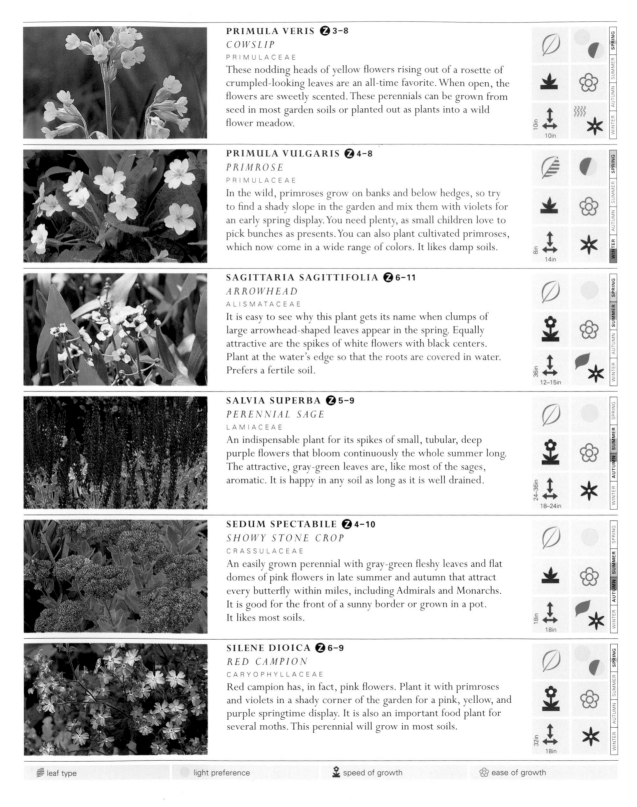

PRIMULA VERIS Z 3–8

COWSLIP

PRIMULACEAE

These nodding heads of yellow flowers rising out of a rosette of crumpled-looking leaves are an all-time favorite. When open, the flowers are sweetly scented. These perennials can be grown from seed in most garden soils or planted out as plants into a wild flower meadow.

PRIMULA VULGARIS Z 4–8

PRIMROSE

PRIMULACEAE

In the wild, primroses grow on banks and below hedges, so try to find a shady slope in the garden and mix them with violets for an early spring display. You need plenty, as small children love to pick bunches as presents. You can also plant cultivated primroses, which now come in a wide range of colors. It likes damp soils.

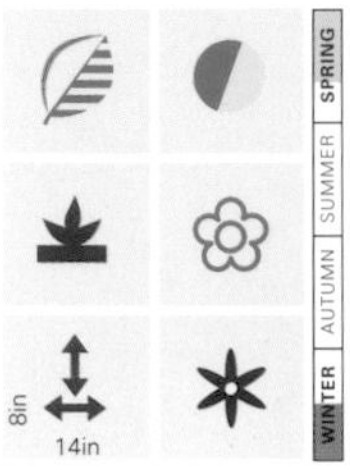

SAGITTARIA SAGITTIFOLIA Z 6–11

ARROWHEAD

ALISMATACEAE

It is easy to see why this plant gets its name when clumps of large arrowhead-shaped leaves appear in the spring. Equally attractive are the spikes of white flowers with black centers. Plant at the water's edge so that the roots are covered in water. Prefers a fertile soil.

SALVIA SUPERBA Z 5–9

PERENNIAL SAGE

LAMIACEAE

An indispensable plant for its spikes of small, tubular, deep purple flowers that bloom continuously the whole summer long. The attractive, gray-green leaves are, like most of the sages, aromatic. It is happy in any soil as long as it is well drained.

SEDUM SPECTABILE Z 4–10

SHOWY STONE CROP

CRASSULACEAE

An easily grown perennial with gray-green fleshy leaves and flat domes of pink flowers in late summer and autumn that attract every butterfly within miles, including Admirals and Monarchs. It is good for the front of a sunny border or grown in a pot. It likes most soils.

SILENE DIOICA Z 6–9

RED CAMPION

CARYOPHYLLACEAE

Red campion has, in fact, pink flowers. Plant it with primroses and violets in a shady corner of the garden for a pink, yellow, and purple springtime display. It is also an important food plant for several moths. This perennial will grow in most soils.

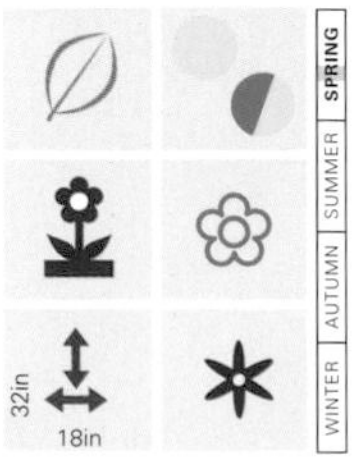

leaf type | light preference | speed of growth | ease of growth

SOLIDAGO CANADENSIS ❷3-10

GOLDEN ROD

ASTERACEAE

A tough, easily grown plant with spikes of yellow flowers in late summer. The old taller golden rods were rather dull, but there are new dwarf varieties like 'Golden Thumb' which is only 1ft (30cm) high and a good front-of-border plant. The flowers are visited by bees and butterflies. Grow in sandy, well-drained soil.

1–6ft
8–15in

TRADESCANTIA X ANDERSONIANA ❷5-9

SPIDERWORT

COMMELINACEAE

An old country-garden plant with tall, arching, straplike foliage and odd three-cornered blue, purple, or white flowers that nestle in the leaves and give it another name, "Moses in the bulrushes". Easy to grow in any soil, they flower right through the summer.

16–24in
18–24in

VERONICA BECCABUNGA ❷5-11

BROOKLIME

SCROPHULARIACEAE

A pretty, low-growing plant that grows in shallow water or wet soil. The bright blue flowers appear throughout the summer and are attractive to honey bees. Sow seeds in wet soil or plant rooted stems. It looks most attractive as ground cover beneath taller waterside plants.

4in
spreads

VERONICA SPICATA ❷3-8

SPIKED SPEEDWELL

SCROPHULARIACEAE

A plant with clumps of shiny green leaves and tall spikes of bright blue flowers, it is easy to grow given a sunny spot and well-drained soil. There are several cultivars, including the subspecies *incana,* with silvery-gray leaves. Like most of the veronicas, it is an excellent bee plant.

12–24in
18in

VIOLA RIVINIANA ❷5-8

VIOLET

VIOLACEAE

The true violets are well worth finding for children to grow. Once planted, they quickly form a carpet of bright green leaves and deep violet flowers. These perennials are a major food plant for the larvae of several fritillary butterflies. They like most soils.

4–8in
8–16in

VIOLA TRICOLOR ❷4-8

JOHNNY-JUMP-UP

VIOLACEAE

Also known as Heartsease, this is a lovely plant for children, producing flowers with pansy "faces" from spring through to autumn. The flowers are usually purple and yellow, but vary in color when grown from seed. Very easy to grow, it is best to treat as an annual and sow new seed every year. It likes any soil.

3–5in
4–6in

SPRING SUMMER AUTUMN WINTER

⇕ height and spread   ✳ feature of interest   ▭ season of interest   *HERBACEOUS PERENNIALS* **P – V**

SHRUBS

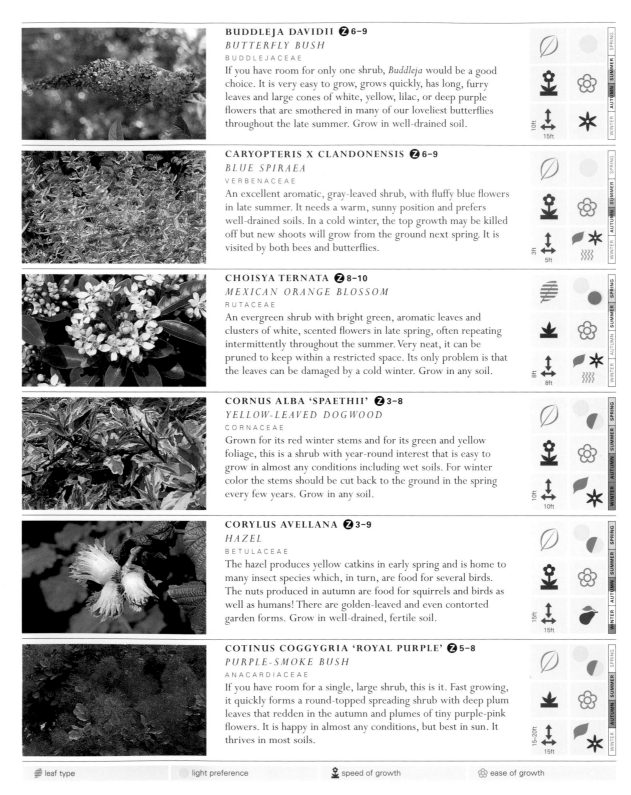

BUDDLEJA DAVIDII ⓩ 6–9
BUTTERFLY BUSH
BUDDLEJACEAE

If you have room for only one shrub, *Buddleja* would be a good choice. It is very easy to grow, grows quickly, has long, furry leaves and large cones of white, yellow, lilac, or deep purple flowers that are smothered in many of our loveliest butterflies throughout the late summer. Grow in well-drained soil.

CARYOPTERIS X CLANDONENSIS ⓩ 6–9
BLUE SPIRAEA
VERBENACEAE

An excellent aromatic, gray-leaved shrub, with fluffy blue flowers in late summer. It needs a warm, sunny position and prefers well-drained soils. In a cold winter, the top growth may be killed off but new shoots will grow from the ground next spring. It is visited by both bees and butterflies.

CHOISYA TERNATA ⓩ 8–10
MEXICAN ORANGE BLOSSOM
RUTACEAE

An evergreen shrub with bright green, aromatic leaves and clusters of white, scented flowers in late spring, often repeating intermittently throughout the summer. Very neat, it can be pruned to keep within a restricted space. Its only problem is that the leaves can be damaged by a cold winter. Grow in any soil.

CORNUS ALBA 'SPAETHII' ⓩ 3–8
YELLOW-LEAVED DOGWOOD
CORNACEAE

Grown for its red winter stems and for its green and yellow foliage, this is a shrub with year-round interest that is easy to grow in almost any conditions including wet soils. For winter color the stems should be cut back to the ground in the spring every few years. Grow in any soil.

CORYLUS AVELLANA ⓩ 3–9
HAZEL
BETULACEAE

The hazel produces yellow catkins in early spring and is home to many insect species which, in turn, are food for several birds. The nuts produced in autumn are food for squirrels and birds as well as humans! There are golden-leaved and even contorted garden forms. Grow in well-drained, fertile soil.

COTINUS COGGYGRIA 'ROYAL PURPLE' ⓩ 5–8
PURPLE-SMOKE BUSH
ANACARDIACEAE

If you have room for a single, large shrub, this is it. Fast growing, it quickly forms a round-topped spreading shrub with deep plum leaves that redden in the autumn and plumes of tiny purple-pink flowers. It is happy in almost any conditions, but best in sun. It thrives in most soils.

leaf type   light preference   speed of growth   ease of growth

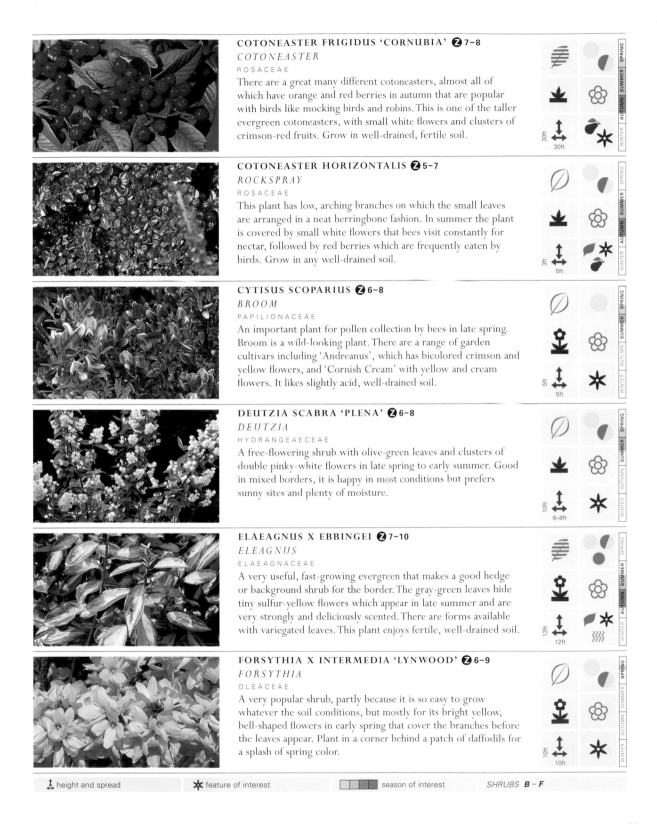

COTONEASTER FRIGIDUS 'CORNUBIA' **Z** 7–8
COTONEASTER
ROSACEAE

There are a great many different cotoneasters, almost all of which have orange and red berries in autumn that are popular with birds like mocking birds and robins. This is one of the taller evergreen cotoneasters, with small white flowers and clusters of crimson-red fruits. Grow in well-drained, fertile soil.

COTONEASTER HORIZONTALIS **Z** 5–7
ROCKSPRAY
ROSACEAE

This plant has low, arching branches on which the small leaves are arranged in a neat herringbone fashion. In summer the plant is covered by small white flowers that bees visit constantly for nectar, followed by red berries which are frequently eaten by birds. Grow in any well-drained soil.

CYTISUS SCOPARIUS **Z** 6–8
BROOM
PAPILIONACEAE

An important plant for pollen collection by bees in late spring. Broom is a wild-looking plant. There are a range of garden cultivars including 'Andreanus', which has bicolored crimson and yellow flowers, and 'Cornish Cream' with yellow and cream flowers. It likes slightly acid, well-drained soil.

DEUTZIA SCABRA 'PLENA' **Z** 6–8
DEUTZIA
HYDRANGEAECEAE

A free-flowering shrub with olive-green leaves and clusters of double pinky-white flowers in late spring to early summer. Good in mixed borders, it is happy in most conditions but prefers sunny sites and plenty of moisture.

ELAEAGNUS X EBBINGEI **Z** 7–10
ELEAGNUS
ELAEAGNACEAE

A very useful, fast-growing evergreen that makes a good hedge or background shrub for the border. The gray-green leaves hide tiny sulfur-yellow flowers which appear in late summer and are very strongly and deliciously scented. There are forms available with variegated leaves. This plant enjoys fertile, well-drained soil.

FORSYTHIA X INTERMEDIA 'LYNWOOD' **Z** 6–9
FORSYTHIA
OLEACEAE

A very popular shrub, partly because it is so easy to grow whatever the soil conditions, but mostly for its bright yellow, bell-shaped flowers in early spring that cover the branches before the leaves appear. Plant in a corner behind a patch of daffodils for a splash of spring color.

↕ height and spread   ✳ feature of interest   ▭ season of interest   *SHRUBS* **B – F**

SHRUBS

FUCHSIA 'RICCARTONII' ❷ 8–10
FUCHSIA

ONAGRACEAE

A firm favorite with children, who love popping the fat buds and making "ballerinas" from the open flowers. A hardy fuchsia, with scarlet and violet flowers through the late summer and autumn. "Mrs Popple" has slightly larger, rather more "poppable" buds. Grow in fertile, well-drained soil.

HEBE 'AUTUMN GLORY' ❷ 9–10
SHRUBBY VERONICA

SCROPHULARIACEAE

One of the best tender shrubs. It forms neat rounded bushes with evergreen, purplish-green leaves and rounded clusters of deep purple flowers throughout the summer. All hebes are attractive to bees and many butterflies. Grow in poor to moderate, moist, but well-drained soil.

MAHONIA AQUIFOLIUM ❷ 6–9
OREGON GRAPE

BERBERIDACEAE

A useful evergreen shrub with dark green, hollylike leaves that turn purple-red in autumn, and bright yellow flowers in early spring. It spreads easily to form a carpet beneath other trees and shrubs. In autumn, blue-black berries are produced. Grow in soil that is moderately fertile, moist, but well-drained.

PEROVSKIA ATRIPLICIFOLIA ❷ 6–9
RUSSIAN SAGE

LAMIACEAE

A sun-loving shrub with gray-green, aromatic, deeply divided leaves, and spikes of lavender-blue in late summer. May suffer in a cold winter but will produce new shoots from the base. Plant in well-drained soil in the middle or back of the border. Popular with bees gathering nectar.

PHILADELPHUS 'BELLE ETOILE' ❷ 5–8
MOCK ORANGE

HYDRANGEACEAE

Mock oranges are unequalled for summer scent, a single bush being capable of scenting all of a small garden. 'Belle Etoile' is one of the best to grow, being a medium-sized shrub with white, single flowers with a maroon blotch and a wonderful fragrance. Grow in any moderately fertile, well-drained soil.

POTENTILLA FRUTICOSA ❷ 3–7
SHRUBBY CINQUEFOIL

ROSACEAE

This is a low, rounded shrub with tiny leaves and a mass of small, single, saucer-shaped flowers in a wide range of colors throughout the summer. Easy to grow in most soils, it prefers a sunny position; its only drawback is that it is uninteresting when not in flower.

≣ leaf type   ◕ light preference   🌱 speed of growth   ✿ ease of growth

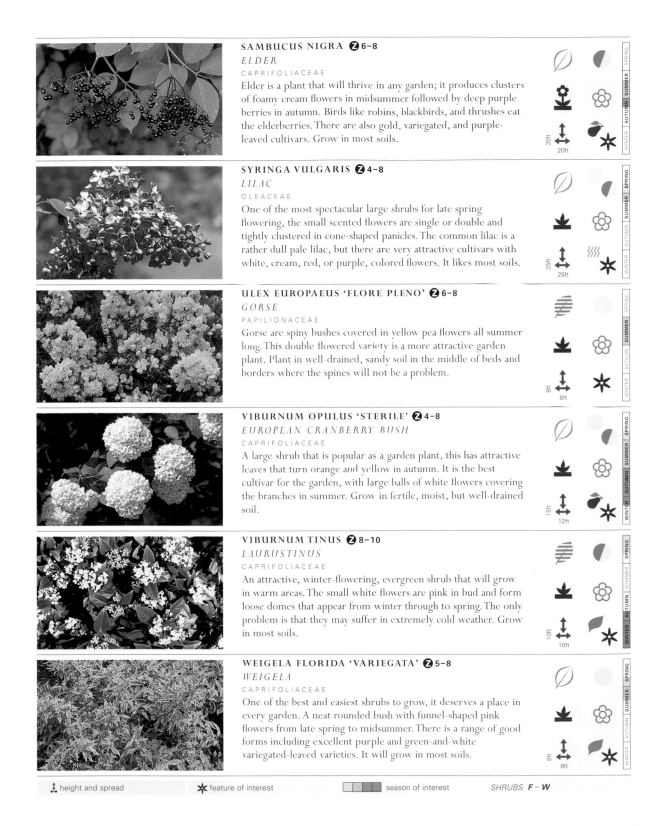

SAMBUCUS NIGRA ❷ 6–8

ELDER

CAPRIFOLIACEAE

Elder is a plant that will thrive in any garden; it produces clusters of foamy cream flowers in midsummer followed by deep purple berries in autumn. Birds like robins, blackbirds, and thrushes eat the elderberries. There are also gold, variegated, and purple-leaved cultivars. Grow in most soils.

20ft
20ft

SYRINGA VULGARIS ❷ 4–8

LILAC

OLEACEAE

One of the most spectacular large shrubs for late spring flowering, the small scented flowers are single or double and tightly clustered in cone-shaped panicles. The common lilac is a rather dull pale lilac, but there are very attractive cultivars with white, cream, red, or purple, colored flowers. It likes most soils.

25ft
25ft

ULEX EUROPAEUS 'FLORE PLENO' ❷ 6–8

GORSE

PAPILIONACEAE

Gorse are spiny bushes covered in yellow pea flowers all summer long. This double flowered variety is a more attractive garden plant. Plant in well-drained, sandy soil in the middle of beds and borders where the spines will not be a problem.

8ft
6ft

VIBURNUM OPULUS 'STERILE' ❷ 4–8

EUROPEAN CRANBERRY BUSH

CAPRIFOLIACEAE

A large shrub that is popular as a garden plant, this has attractive leaves that turn orange and yellow in autumn. It is the best cultivar for the garden, with large balls of white flowers covering the branches in summer. Grow in fertile, moist, but well-drained soil.

15ft
12ft

VIBURNUM TINUS ❷ 8–10

LAURUSTINUS

CAPRIFOLIACEAE

An attractive, winter-flowering, evergreen shrub that will grow in warm areas. The small white flowers are pink in bud and form loose domes that appear from winter through to spring. The only problem is that they may suffer in extremely cold weather. Grow in most soils.

10ft
10ft

WEIGELA FLORIDA 'VARIEGATA' ❷ 5–8

WEIGELA

CAPRIFOLIACEAE

One of the best and easiest shrubs to grow, it deserves a place in every garden. A neat rounded bush with funnel-shaped pink flowers from late spring to midsummer. There is a range of good forms including excellent purple and green-and-white variegated-leaved varieties. It will grow in most soils.

8ft
8ft

⬍ height and spread   ✳ feature of interest   ▭ season of interest   *SHRUBS* **F – W**

ROSES

ROSA 'FLOWER CARPET' ❷ 5-9
ROSE
ROSACEAE

A great rose for the novice gardener as it seems to grow unaffected by any of the pests and diseases that damage other roses. It has shiny, almost evergreen leaves, low spreading branches, and bright pink flowers for most of the summer. Try it in a large pot on the patio. Grows in most soils.

ROSA 'GRAHAM THOMAS' ❷ 5-9
ROSE
ROSACEAE

The English roses need less pruning and general care than the Floribunda and Hybrid Teas, but have the same large flowers and flower continuously. 'Graham Thomas' has large, cupped, double, deep yellow flowers with a rich, old rose fragrance and is one of the most reliable of the English roses. Grows in most soils.

ROSA 'ICEBERG' ❷ 5-9
ROSE
ROSACEAE

The finest and best white Floribunda rose, with clusters of pink-tinged buds opening to lightly scented white flowers, and glossy green leaves that can stay on the bushes into the winter. Flowers throughout the summer, and its only needs are an annual light prune, a little food, and the occasional spray. Grows in most soils.

ROSA 'JUST JOEY' ❷ 5-9
ROSE
ROSACEAE

One of the very best Hybrid Tea roses, 'Just Joey' is almost perfect, with large, fragrant, coppery-orange flowers from early summer to late autumn, and dark green, disease-resistant foliage. Like all Hybrid Teas, it needs annual pruning and feeding, and may need spraying from time to time. Grows in most soils.

ROSA 'NEVADA' ❷ 4-9
ROSE
ROSACEAE

To really enjoy 'Nevada' at its best you need plenty of room. It needs at least 10ft (3m), but the reward is a rounded bush of elegantly arching branches covered in large, creamy blooms in June and September. It needs no pruning and infrequent spraying. Grows in most soils.

ROSA 'PENELOPE' ❷ 6-9
ROSE
ROSACEAE

'Penelope' has everything you could want in a rose except small size: it needs to be allowed to grow unpruned to show its true potential, which is large clusters of semidouble, palest pink, beautifully scented flowers that repeat flower from June to November, and disease-resistant shiny leaves. It likes most soils.

≋ leaf type	● light preference	♠ speed of growth	❁ ease of growth

CONIFERS

CHAMAECYPARIS LAWSONIANA 'PEMBURY BLUE'
LAWSON'S CYPRESS **Z** 5–9
CUPRESSACEAE

Probably the easiest of the "blue" conifers to grow, Lawson's cypress is not fussy about soil, and grows relatively quickly. 'Pembury Blue' has neat, silvery-blue foliage, and initially forms an upright bush that develops into a columnar tree. It will tolerate most soils.

50ft · 6–15ft

CHAMAECYPARIS PISIFERA 'BOULEVARD' **Z** 4–8
SAWARA CYPRESS
CUPRESSACEAE

Usually bought as a dwarf conifer, 'Boulevard' can ultimately grow to over 13ft (4m)! The steel-blue foliage is more open and feathery than 'Pembury Blue' and the plant grows into a more globular shape. Easy to grow, its preference is for moist soils that are not too heavy.

13ft · 10ft

CRYPTOMERIA JAPONICA 'ELEGANS' **Z** 6–9
JAPANESE CEDAR
TAXODIACEAE

A conifer that merits a place in the shrub border for its attractive green foliage that turns copper-bronze during the winter. It also makes a good specimen tree or container plant, remaining attractive throughout the year. It is easy to grow in all but very dry conditions. Grow in any well-drained soil.

20–30ft · 5–10ft

JUNIPERUS X PFITZERIANA **Z** 4–9
PFITZER JUNIPER
CUPRESSACEAE

Not for very small gardens, but a wonderful architectural ground covering conifer where there is space. Not fussy as to soil, it is, unlike many other conifers, happy in shade. One word of warning: the plant is prickly to touch and so best positioned where children will not reach it. Grow in any well-drained soil.

4ft · 10ft

THUJA OCCIDENTALIS 'RHEINGOLD' **Z** 2–7
AMERICAN ARBORVITAE
CUPRESSACEAE

If you want a golden conifer, 'Rheingold' is your best choice, with old-gold-colored foliage turning a rich copper-gold in winter, which adds a warmth to even the coldest garden. The arborvitae is a very tolerant, easy-to-grow conifer, but prefers soils that are not too wet.

3–6ft · 3–6ft

THUJA PLICATA 'ZEBRINA' **Z** 6–8
WESTERN RED CEDAR
CUPRESSACEAE

This is another easy-to-grow, vigorous conifer that eventually makes a large tree. The foliage is light green striped with yellow-green and makes an interesting specimen plant for medium to large gardens. It tolerates almost all soils and conditions, including high alkalinity and extreme cold.

40–50ft · 12ft

↕ height and spread   ✳ feature of interest   ▮▮▮ season of interest   *ROSES, CONIFERS*

CLIMBERS

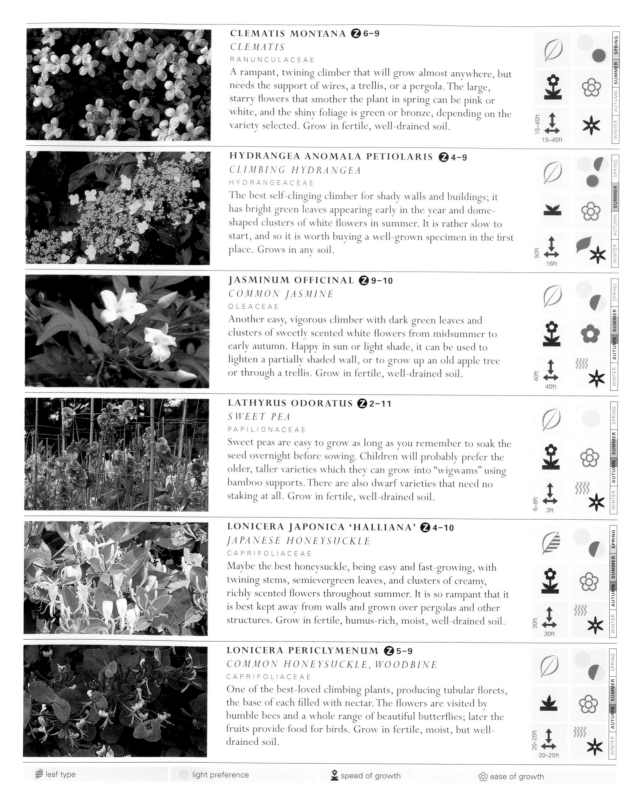

CLEMATIS MONTANA ❷ 6–9
CLEMATIS
RANUNCULACEAE

A rampant, twining climber that will grow almost anywhere, but needs the support of wires, a trellis, or a pergola. The large, starry flowers that smother the plant in spring can be pink or white, and the shiny foliage is green or bronze, depending on the variety selected. Grow in fertile, well-drained soil.

15–45ft
15–45ft

HYDRANGEA ANOMALA PETIOLARIS ❷ 4–9
CLIMBING HYDRANGEA
HYDRANGEACEAE

The best self-clinging climber for shady walls and buildings; it has bright green leaves appearing early in the year and dome-shaped clusters of white flowers in summer. It is rather slow to start, and so it is worth buying a well-grown specimen in the first place. Grows in any soil.

50ft
16ft

JASMINUM OFFICINAL ❷ 9–10
COMMON JASMINE
OLEACEAE

Another easy, vigorous climber with dark green leaves and clusters of sweetly scented white flowers from midsummer to early autumn. Happy in sun or light shade, it can be used to lighten a partially shaded wall, or to grow up an old apple tree or through a trellis. Grow in fertile, well-drained soil.

40ft
40ft

LATHYRUS ODORATUS ❷ 2–11
SWEET PEA
PAPILIONACEAE

Sweet peas are easy to grow as long as you remember to soak the seed overnight before sowing. Children will probably prefer the older, taller varieties which they can grow into "wigwams" using bamboo supports. There are also dwarf varieties that need no staking at all. Grow in fertile, well-drained soil.

6–8ft
3ft

LONICERA JAPONICA 'HALLIANA' ❷ 4–10
JAPANESE HONEYSUCKLE
CAPRIFOLIACEAE

Maybe the best honeysuckle, being easy and fast-growing, with twining stems, semievergreen leaves, and clusters of creamy, richly scented flowers throughout summer. It is so rampant that it is best kept away from walls and grown over pergolas and other structures. Grow in fertile, humus-rich, moist, well-drained soil.

30ft
30ft

LONICERA PERICLYMENUM ❷ 5–9
COMMON HONEYSUCKLE, WOODBINE
CAPRIFOLIACEAE

One of the best-loved climbing plants, producing tubular florets, the base of each filled with nectar. The flowers are visited by bumble bees and a whole range of beautiful butterflies; later the fruits provide food for birds. Grow in fertile, moist, but well-drained soil.

20–25ft
20–25ft

SPRING | SUMMER | AUTUMN | WINTER

leaf type   light preference   speed of growth   ease of growth

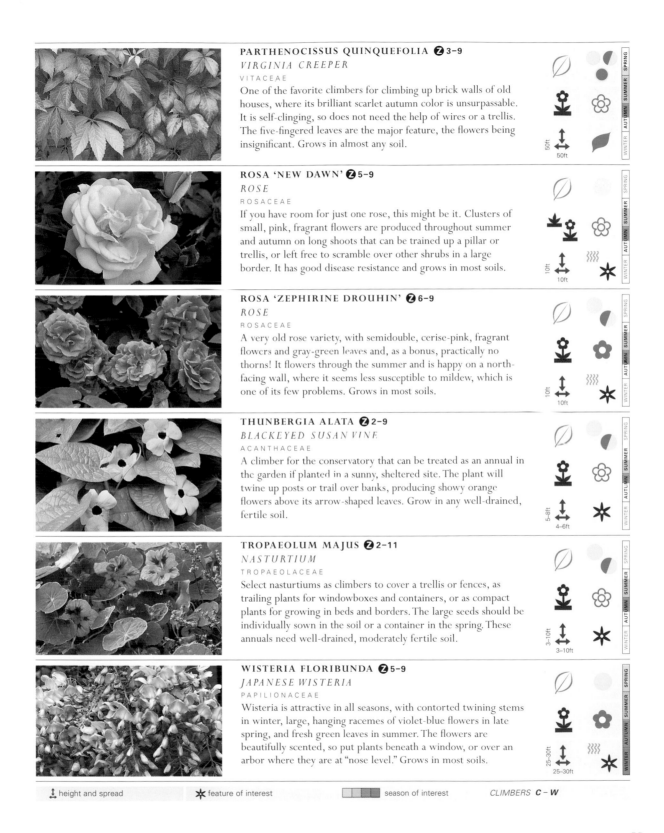

PARTHENOCISSUS QUINQUEFOLIA **ⓩ 3–9**
VIRGINIA CREEPER
VITACEAE

One of the favorite climbers for climbing up brick walls of old houses, where its brilliant scarlet autumn color is unsurpassable. It is self-clinging, so does not need the help of wires or a trellis. The five-fingered leaves are the major feature, the flowers being insignificant. Grows in almost any soil.

50ft
50ft

ROSA 'NEW DAWN' **ⓩ 5–9**
ROSE
ROSACEAE

If you have room for just one rose, this might be it. Clusters of small, pink, fragrant flowers are produced throughout summer and autumn on long shoots that can be trained up a pillar or trellis, or left free to scramble over other shrubs in a large border. It has good disease resistance and grows in most soils.

10ft
10ft

ROSA 'ZEPHIRINE DROUHIN' **ⓩ 6–9**
ROSE
ROSACEAE

A very old rose variety, with semidouble, cerise-pink, fragrant flowers and gray-green leaves and, as a bonus, practically no thorns! It flowers through the summer and is happy on a north-facing wall, where it seems less susceptible to mildew, which is one of its few problems. Grows in most soils.

10ft
10ft

THUNBERGIA ALATA **ⓩ 2–9**
BLACKEYED SUSAN VINE
ACANTHACEAE

A climber for the conservatory that can be treated as an annual in the garden if planted in a sunny, sheltered site. The plant will twine up posts or trail over banks, producing showy orange flowers above its arrow-shaped leaves. Grow in any well-drained, fertile soil.

5–8ft
4–6ft

TROPAEOLUM MAJUS **ⓩ 2–11**
NASTURTIUM
TROPAEOLACEAE

Select nasturtiums as climbers to cover a trellis or fences, as trailing plants for windowboxes and containers, or as compact plants for growing in beds and borders. The large seeds should be individually sown in the soil or a container in the spring. These annuals need well-drained, moderately fertile soil.

3–10ft
3–10ft

WISTERIA FLORIBUNDA **ⓩ 5–9**
JAPANESE WISTERIA
PAPILIONACEAE

Wisteria is attractive in all seasons, with contorted twining stems in winter, large, hanging racemes of violet-blue flowers in late spring, and fresh green leaves in summer. The flowers are beautifully scented, so put plants beneath a window, or over an arbor where they are at "nose level." Grows in most soils.

25–30ft
25–30ft

⌀ height and spread　　✳ feature of interest　　▮▮▮ season of interest　　*CLIMBERS C – W*

TREES

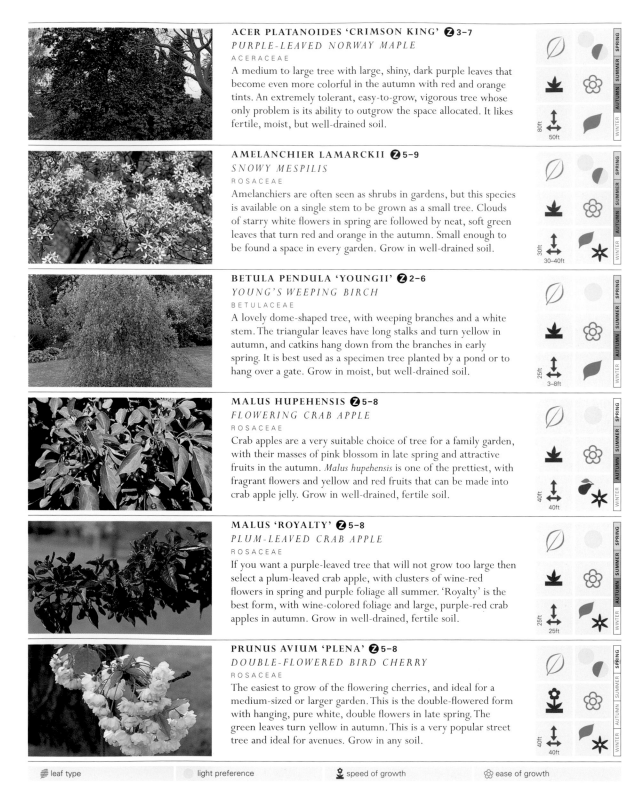

ACER PLATANOIDES 'CRIMSON KING' Z 3–7
PURPLE-LEAVED NORWAY MAPLE
ACERACEAE

A medium to large tree with large, shiny, dark purple leaves that become even more colorful in the autumn with red and orange tints. An extremely tolerant, easy-to-grow, vigorous tree whose only problem is its ability to outgrow the space allocated. It likes fertile, moist, but well-drained soil.

80ft / 50ft

AMELANCHIER LAMARCKII Z 5–9
SNOWY MESPILIS
ROSACEAE

Amelanchiers are often seen as shrubs in gardens, but this species is available on a single stem to be grown as a small tree. Clouds of starry white flowers in spring are followed by neat, soft green leaves that turn red and orange in the autumn. Small enough to be found a space in every garden. Grow in well-drained soil.

30ft / 30–40ft

BETULA PENDULA 'YOUNGII' Z 2–6
YOUNG'S WEEPING BIRCH
BETULACEAE

A lovely dome-shaped tree, with weeping branches and a white stem. The triangular leaves have long stalks and turn yellow in autumn, and catkins hang down from the branches in early spring. It is best used as a specimen tree planted by a pond or to hang over a gate. Grow in moist, but well-drained soil.

25ft / 3–8ft

MALUS HUPEHENSIS Z 5–8
FLOWERING CRAB APPLE
ROSACEAE

Crab apples are a very suitable choice of tree for a family garden, with their masses of pink blossom in late spring and attractive fruits in the autumn. *Malus hupehensis* is one of the prettiest, with fragrant flowers and yellow and red fruits that can be made into crab apple jelly. Grow in well-drained, fertile soil.

40ft / 40ft

MALUS 'ROYALTY' Z 5–8
PLUM-LEAVED CRAB APPLE
ROSACEAE

If you want a purple-leaved tree that will not grow too large then select a plum-leaved crab apple, with clusters of wine-red flowers in spring and purple foliage all summer. 'Royalty' is the best form, with wine-colored foliage and large, purple-red crab apples in autumn. Grow in well-drained, fertile soil.

25ft / 25ft

PRUNUS AVIUM 'PLENA' Z 5–8
DOUBLE-FLOWERED BIRD CHERRY
ROSACEAE

The easiest to grow of the flowering cherries, and ideal for a medium-sized or larger garden. This is the double-flowered form with hanging, pure white, double flowers in late spring. The green leaves turn yellow in autumn. This is a very popular street tree and ideal for avenues. Grow in any soil.

40ft / 40ft

SPRING | SUMMER | AUTUMN | WINTER

≣ leaf type   ● light preference   ♟ speed of growth   ✿ ease of growth

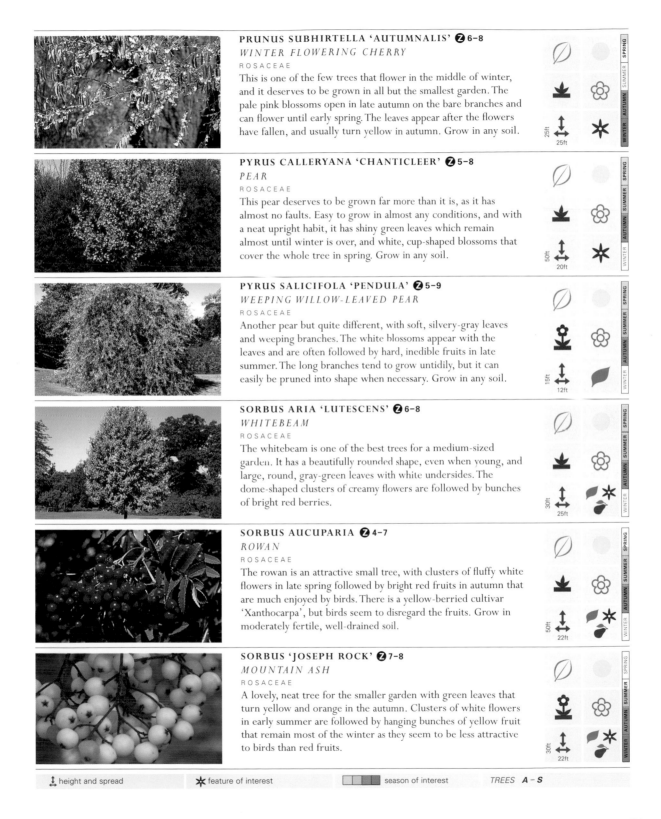

PRUNUS SUBHIRTELLA 'AUTUMNALIS' ⓩ 6–8
WINTER FLOWERING CHERRY
ROSACEAE
This is one of the few trees that flower in the middle of winter, and it deserves to be grown in all but the smallest garden. The pale pink blossoms open in late autumn on the bare branches and can flower until early spring. The leaves appear after the flowers have fallen, and usually turn yellow in autumn. Grow in any soil.

25ft / 25ft

PYRUS CALLERYANA 'CHANTICLEER' ⓩ 5–8
PEAR
ROSACEAE
This pear deserves to be grown far more than it is, as it has almost no faults. Easy to grow in almost any conditions, and with a neat upright habit, it has shiny green leaves which remain almost until winter is over, and white, cup-shaped blossoms that cover the whole tree in spring. Grow in any soil.

50ft / 20ft

PYRUS SALICIFOLA 'PENDULA' ⓩ 5–9
WEEPING WILLOW-LEAVED PEAR
ROSACEAE
Another pear but quite different, with soft, silvery-gray leaves and weeping branches. The white blossoms appear with the leaves and are often followed by hard, inedible fruits in late summer. The long branches tend to grow untidily, but it can easily be pruned into shape when necessary. Grow in any soil.

15ft / 12ft

SORBUS ARIA 'LUTESCENS' ⓩ 6–8
WHITEBEAM
ROSACEAE
The whitebeam is one of the best trees for a medium-sized garden. It has a beautifully rounded shape, even when young, and large, round, gray-green leaves with white undersides. The dome-shaped clusters of creamy flowers are followed by bunches of bright red berries.

30ft / 25ft

SORBUS AUCUPARIA ⓩ 4–7
ROWAN
ROSACEAE
The rowan is an attractive small tree, with clusters of fluffy white flowers in late spring followed by bright red fruits in autumn that are much enjoyed by birds. There is a yellow-berried cultivar 'Xanthocarpa', but birds seem to disregard the fruits. Grow in moderately fertile, well-drained soil.

50ft / 22ft

SORBUS 'JOSEPH ROCK' ⓩ 7–8
MOUNTAIN ASH
ROSACEAE
A lovely, neat tree for the smaller garden with green leaves that turn yellow and orange in the autumn. Clusters of white flowers in early summer are followed by hanging bunches of yellow fruit that remain most of the winter as they seem to be less attractive to birds than red fruits.

30ft / 22ft

↕ height and spread   ✻ feature of interest   ▭▬ season of interest   *TREES* **A – S**

91

VEGETABLES AND FRUIT

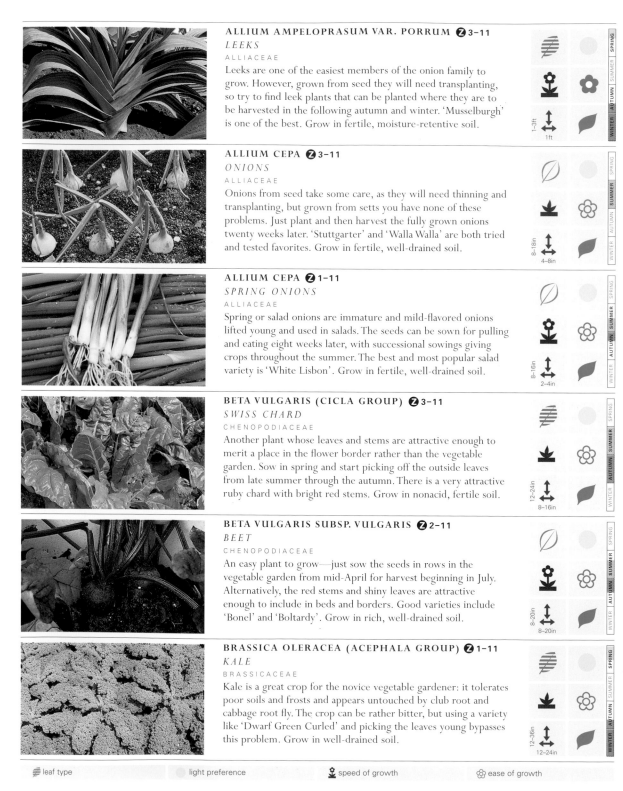

ALLIUM AMPELOPRASUM VAR. PORRUM ⓩ 3–11
LEEKS
ALLIACEAE

Leeks are one of the easiest members of the onion family to grow. However, grown from seed they will need transplanting, so try to find leek plants that can be planted where they are to be harvested in the following autumn and winter. 'Musselburgh' is one of the best. Grow in fertile, moisture-retentive soil.

1–3ft
1ft

ALLIUM CEPA ⓩ 3–11
ONIONS
ALLIACEAE

Onions from seed take some care, as they will need thinning and transplanting, but grown from sets you have none of these problems. Just plant and then harvest the fully grown onions twenty weeks later. 'Stuttgarter' and 'Walla Walla' are both tried and tested favorites. Grow in fertile, well-drained soil.

8–18in
4–8in

ALLIUM CEPA ⓩ 1–11
SPRING ONIONS
ALLIACEAE

Spring or salad onions are immature and mild-flavored onions lifted young and used in salads. The seeds can be sown for pulling and eating eight weeks later, with successional sowings giving crops throughout the summer. The best and most popular salad variety is 'White Lisbon'. Grow in fertile, well-drained soil.

8–16in
2–4in

BETA VULGARIS (CICLA GROUP) ⓩ 3–11
SWISS CHARD
CHENOPODIACEAE

Another plant whose leaves and stems are attractive enough to merit a place in the flower border rather than the vegetable garden. Sow in spring and start picking off the outside leaves from late summer through the autumn. There is a very attractive ruby chard with bright red stems. Grow in nonacid, fertile soil.

12–24in
8–16in

BETA VULGARIS SUBSP. VULGARIS ⓩ 2–11
BEET
CHENOPODIACEAE

An easy plant to grow—just sow the seeds in rows in the vegetable garden from mid-April for harvest beginning in July. Alternatively, the red stems and shiny leaves are attractive enough to include in beds and borders. Good varieties include 'Bonel' and 'Boltardy'. Grow in rich, well-drained soil.

8–20in
8–20in

BRASSICA OLERACEA (ACEPHALA GROUP) ⓩ 1–11
KALE
BRASSICACEAE

Kale is a great crop for the novice vegetable gardener: it tolerates poor soils and frosts and appears untouched by club root and cabbage root fly. The crop can be rather bitter, but using a variety like 'Dwarf Green Curled' and picking the leaves young bypasses this problem. Grow in well-drained soil.

12–36in
12–24in

⬚ leaf type   ⬤ light preference   ⚘ speed of growth   ⚘ ease of growth

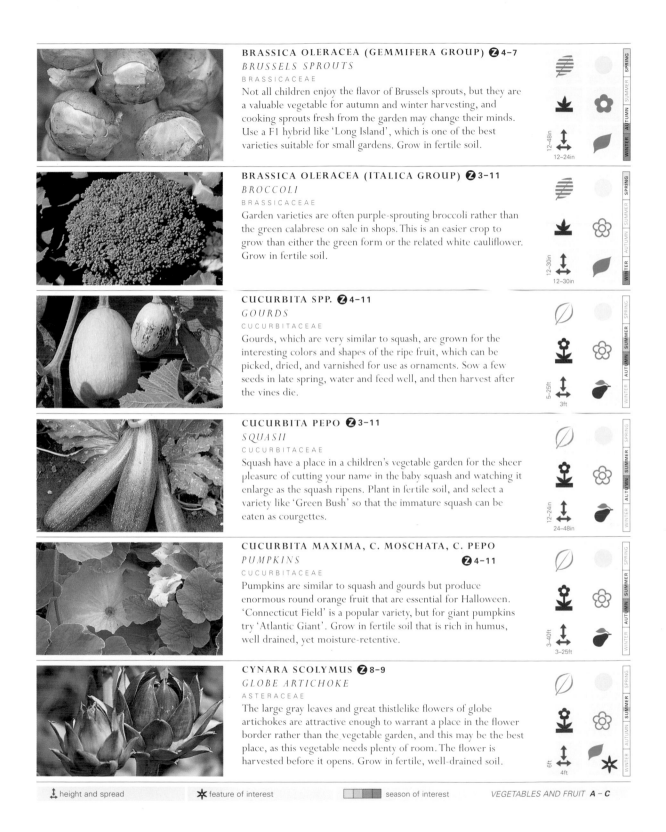

BRASSICA OLERACEA (GEMMIFERA GROUP) ❷4–7
BRUSSELS SPROUTS
BRASSICACEAE
Not all children enjoy the flavor of Brussels sprouts, but they are a valuable vegetable for autumn and winter harvesting, and cooking sprouts fresh from the garden may change their minds. Use a F1 hybrid like 'Long Island', which is one of the best varieties suitable for small gardens. Grow in fertile soil.

12–48in
12–24in

SPRING SUMMER AUTUMN WINTER

BRASSICA OLERACEA (ITALICA GROUP) ❷3–11
BROCCOLI
BRASSICACEAE
Garden varieties are often purple-sprouting broccoli rather than the green calabrese on sale in shops. This is an easier crop to grow than either the green form or the related white cauliflower. Grow in fertile soil.

12–30in
12–30in

SPRING SUMMER AUTUMN WINTER

CUCURBITA SPP. ❷4–11
GOURDS
CUCURBITACEAE
Gourds, which are very similar to squash, are grown for the interesting colors and shapes of the ripe fruit, which can be picked, dried, and varnished for use as ornaments. Sow a few seeds in late spring, water and feed well, and then harvest after the vines die.

5–25ft
3ft

SPRING SUMMER AUTUMN WINTER

CUCURBITA PEPO ❷3–11
SQUASH
CUCURBITACEAE
Squash have a place in a children's vegetable garden for the sheer pleasure of cutting your name in the baby squash and watching it enlarge as the squash ripens. Plant in fertile soil, and select a variety like 'Green Bush' so that the immature squash can be eaten as courgettes.

12–24in
24–48in

SPRING SUMMER AUTUMN WINTER

CUCURBITA MAXIMA, C. MOSCHATA, C. PEPO
PUMPKINS ❷4–11
CUCURBITACEAE
Pumpkins are similar to squash and gourds but produce enormous round orange fruit that are essential for Halloween. 'Connecticut Field' is a popular variety, but for giant pumpkins try 'Atlantic Giant'. Grow in fertile soil that is rich in humus, well drained, yet moisture-retentive.

3–40ft
3–25ft

SPRING SUMMER AUTUMN WINTER

CYNARA SCOLYMUS ❷8–9
GLOBE ARTICHOKE
ASTERACEAE
The large gray leaves and great thistlelike flowers of globe artichokes are attractive enough to warrant a place in the flower border rather than the vegetable garden, and this may be the best place, as this vegetable needs plenty of room. The flower is harvested before it opens. Grow in fertile, well-drained soil.

6ft
4ft

SPRING SUMMER AUTUMN WINTER

↕ height and spread   ✳ feature of interest   ▭▭▭ season of interest   *VEGETABLES AND FRUIT* **A – C**

VEGETABLES AND FRUIT

DAUCUS CAROTA ❷ 3–11
CARROTS
APIACEAE
Carrots are one of the easiest vegetables to grow, with the feathery leaves emerging two weeks after sowing and the carrot roots developing almost as quickly, with fully grown carrots being ready to pull twelve weeks after sowing. Carrots are a good starting crop for impatient young gardeners. Grow in fertile soil.

4–16in
4–12in
SPRING SUMMER AUTUMN WINTER

FRAGARIA VESCA ❷ 2–11
ALPINE STRAWBERRIES
ROSACEAE
These low-growing perennial plants produce small, sweet strawberries throughout the summer; most birds tend to ignore them. Once planted they are easy to grow, and can be left in place for several years. 'Baron Solemacher' is one of the best. Grow in moist, but well-drained, fertile, neutral to alkaline soil.

12in
spreads
SPRING SUMMER AUTUMN WINTER

LACTUCA SATIVA ❷ 1–11
LETTUCE
ASTERACEAE
Lettuce is another good crop for the young impatient gardener, with many of the loose-leaf varieties being cut only six weeks after sowing. Sow any time from late spring through the summer on well-fertilized soil. 'Tom Thumb' is a good, fast-growing small variety, or start with a packet of mixed lettuce seed.

5–25in
5–15in
SPRING SUMMER AUTUMN WINTER

LYCOPERSICON ESCULENTUM ❷ 3–11
TOMATOES
SOLANACEAE
One of the easiest plants to grow, tomatoes are a big favorite for the family garden. Or choose a bushy variety such as 'Little Wonder', which can be grown in a container and does not need supports. Grow in fertile soil—dig in plenty of well-rotted manure before planting.

10–72in
8–24in
SPRING SUMMER AUTUMN WINTER

PHASEOLUS COCCINEUS ❷ 4–11
POLE BEANS
PAPILIONACEAE
Included here for the pleasure of growing up trellises, over playhouses or "wigwams" of bamboo, runner beans are a favorite with most children. The bright red flowers are followed by long bean pods that offer the chance of a competition for growing the longest bean. Grow in fertile soil that retains moisture.

3–15ft
8–10in
SPRING SUMMER AUTUMN WINTER

PHASEOLUS VULGARIS ❷ 3–11
BEANS
PAPILIONACEAE
Ready before pole beans and without the need for supports, beans are a useful and relatively easy plant to grow in the summer vegetable garden. Sow direct as soon as the last frosts are over in any but a heavy clay or acid soil.

8–20in
4–8in
SPRING SUMMER AUTUMN WINTER

≣ leaf type   ● light preference   ♉ speed of growth   ❀ ease of growth

PISUM SATIVUM ❷ 2–11
PEAS
PAPILIONACEAE

The flavor of young, newly shelled peas is deliciously sweet. You can also grow snow or snap peas, which are eaten in the pod and so eliminate the need for shelling. Grow in moisture-retentive, but well-drained soil, and incorporate plenty of well-rotted manure before planting.

12–72in
2–3in

RAPHANUS SATIVUS ❷ 1–11
RADISHES
BRASSICACEAE

Even faster growing than carrots, radishes can be ready for pulling about a month after sowing, and are ideal for children to grow even if they are not absolutely sure about the peppery taste. 'French Breakfast' is an excellent, mild-flavored variety, but needs harvesting young. Grow in rich, well-drained soil.

8–12in
4–8in

RUMEX ACETOSA ❷ 1–11
SORREL
POLYGONACEAE

A good plant to grow as a "cut and come again" salad vegetable. The lemony flavor of the leaves is a delicious addition to salads or soups. A perennial plant, it can be left over winter for cutting in subsequent years or grown annually from seed. It needs a well-drained, fertile soil enriched with added humus.

12–24in
8–12in

SOLANUM TUBEROSUM ❷ 3–11
POTATOES
SOLANACEAE

To keep the family in potatoes all year through requires more space in our gardens than is often available, but they are a useful crop and it is worthwhile at least growing early potatoes. Grow in well-drained, fertile soil that is at least 2ft (60cm) deep.

12–36in
12–36in

VICIA FABA ❷ 3–11
BROAD BEANS
PAPILIONACEAE

A vegetable that the whole family can enjoy growing, with the younger members having fun watching the large seeds germinate and later helping to strip off the beans' "fur" coats. There is a good dwarf variety, 'The Sutton'. Broad beans are not fussy about soil as long as it is well drained. Plant early.

12–36in
12in

ZEA MAYS ❷ 3–11
SWEET CORN
POACEAE

Sweet corn needs to wait for the last of the frosts before sowing, but, given a warm summer, the giant stems grow amazingly quickly, and the tassels of the flowers and the ripening ears are fascinating to young gardeners. The ears should be ready for harvesting fourteen weeks after sowing. Grow in fertile soil.

4–8ft
12–24in

SPRING SUMMER AUTUMN WINTER

⬍ height and spread   ✻ feature of interest   ▭▭▭▭ season of interest   *VEGETABLES AND FRUIT D – Z*

HERBS

ALLIUM SCHOENOPRASUM ❷ 3–9
CHIVES
ALLIACEAE

Chives make an ideal edging to the vegetable plot, with their neat clumps of grasslike leaves and round heads of pink flowers. Add the onion-flavored leaves to soups, salads, and sandwiches, and use the flowers to decorate salads. Sow seeds direct or use small plants. Grow in well-drained or moist soil.

ANETHUM GRAVEOLENS ❷ 2–9
DILL
APIACEAE

The fine feathery leaves and small yellow-green flowers look like fennel, and if grown together the two plants may hybridize. Sow the seeds into pots or the ground where the crop is to grow, and cut fresh leaves to use with fish dishes or harvest the seeds to add to pickling vinegar. Grow in a fertile, well-drained soil.

ANGELICA ARCHANGELICA ❷ 4–9
ANGELICA
APIACEAE

With large cut leaves and elegant stems carrying round balls of flowers, angelica is a plant that makes a statement wherever it is planted. The young cut stems make a crystallized cake decoration, and the leaves and stems can be stewed with fruit. Finches love to eat the seeds. Grow deep in moist, fertile soil.

ANTHRISCUS CEREFOLIUM ❷ 3–7
CHERVIL
APIACEAE

A hardy annual which, if sown late in the summer in warmer areas, acts as a biennial and will provide leaves for cutting in the winter, before flowering and dying the next year. The fresh green fernlike leaves are cut for use in salads, soups, sauces, and with vegetables. Grow in a well-drained or moist soil.

ARTEMISIA DRACUNCULUS ❷ 3–7
TARRAGON
ASTERACEAE

Not a particularly attractive plant, but a "must" for all cooks. Check that you plant French tarragon and not the Russian form which is larger and practically tasteless. Once established, pick young leaves from the plant for using fresh from June to October. Grow in well-drained, fertile soil.

BORAGO OFFICINALIS ❷ 3–9
BORAGE
BORAGINACEAE

An annual with bright blue, star-shaped flowers and furry leaves and stems that have a cucumberlike flavor. It grows very easily from seed and will happily self-seed and come up year after year. The flowers can be used in salads and summer drinks and are visited by bees for pollen and nectar. Grow in any soil.

≣ leaf type   ● light preference   ⚓ speed of growth   ✿ ease of growth

CARUM CARVI ❷ 3–9
CARAWAY
APIACEAE

This plant has fernlike leaves and small white flowers that produce aromatic seeds which are used to flavor cakes, bread, vegetables, and stews. The roots can be cooked as a vegetable if left to the second autumn after sowing. Easy to grow from seed in any reasonable, well-drained soil.

24in
12in

CORIANDRUM SATIVUM ❷ 2–9
CORIANDER
APIACEAE

An increasingly popular herb with both the leaves and seeds being used in cooking. Sow the seeds in spring or early summer where they are to grow, as coriander dislikes being transplanted. Avoid growing in damp or humid areas as it needs dry conditions to crop well.

20–30in
8–12in

FOENICULUM VULGARE ❷ 4–9
FENNEL
APIACEAE

Fennel forms tall drifts of feathery foliage topped by flat domes of tiny yellow flowers in the late summer. Plant either in a herb garden or at the back of a border. There is a bronze-leaved cultivar, 'Purpureum', that is even more attractive and just as useful in the kitchen. Grow in fertile, moist, well-drained soil.

6ft
18in

HYSSOPUS OFFICINALIS ❷ 6–9
HYSSOP
LAMIACEAE

A very pretty herb with upright stems of aromatic dark green leaves and spikes of blue or pink flowers. Traditionally used in the treatment of whooping cough and chest ailments, it is now used as an edging plant or a low hedge. Popular with both butterflies and bees. Grow in fertile, well-drained soil.

24in
36in

LAURUS NOBILIS ❷ 8–10
SWEET BAY
LAURACEAE

A large evergreen plant that can be trained to form a mop-headed tree, clipped as a rounded bush, or left unclipped to grow into a tree or large shrub. There is a golden-leaved cultivar, 'Aureum', that can be used to brighten up a shady corner. The leaves of both can be used in cooking. Grow in fertile, moist, but well-drained soil.

40ft
30ft

LAVANDULA ANGUSTIFOLIA ❷ 5–8
LAVENDER
LAMIACEAE

There are lots of different lavenders for the gardener to grow, and all form rounded bushes with spikes of aromatic flowers in all shades of lavender blue, but also white and pink. It is a very important plant for both bees and butterflies. All varieties need well-drained, preferably limey soil in full sun.

3ft
4ft

⬍ height and spread   ✳ feature of interest   ▭▭▭▭ season of interest   *HERBS A – L*

HERBS

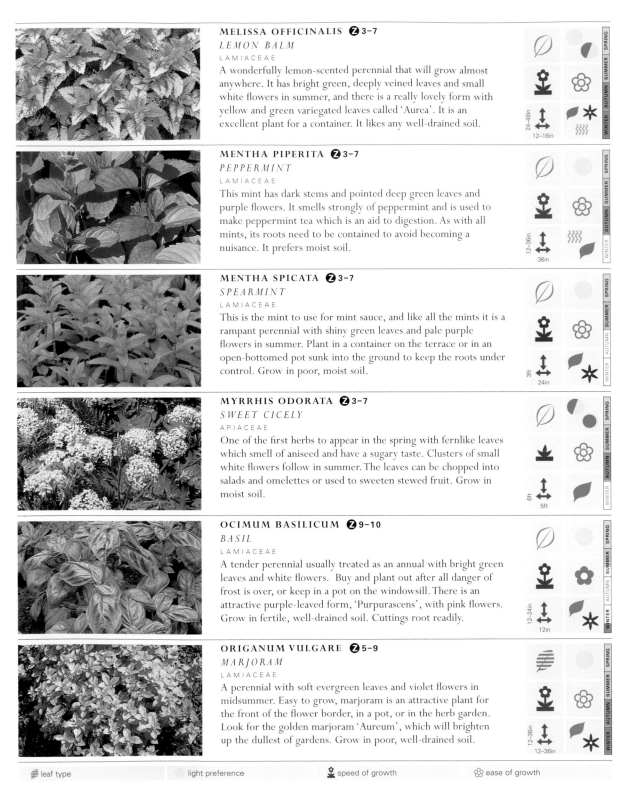

MELISSA OFFICINALIS ⓩ 3–7

LEMON BALM

LAMIACEAE

A wonderfully lemon-scented perennial that will grow almost anywhere. It has bright green, deeply veined leaves and small white flowers in summer, and there is a really lovely form with yellow and green variegated leaves called 'Aurea'. It is an excellent plant for a container. It likes any well-drained soil.

24–48in
12–18in

MENTHA PIPERITA ⓩ 3–7

PEPPERMINT

LAMIACEAE

This mint has dark stems and pointed deep green leaves and purple flowers. It smells strongly of peppermint and is used to make peppermint tea which is an aid to digestion. As with all mints, its roots need to be contained to avoid becoming a nuisance. It prefers moist soil.

12–36in
36in

MENTHA SPICATA ⓩ 3–7

SPEARMINT

LAMIACEAE

This is the mint to use for mint sauce, and like all the mints it is a rampant perennial with shiny green leaves and pale purple flowers in summer. Plant in a container on the terrace or in an open-bottomed pot sunk into the ground to keep the roots under control. Grow in poor, moist soil.

3ft
24in

MYRRHIS ODORATA ⓩ 3–7

SWEET CICELY

APIACEAE

One of the first herbs to appear in the spring with fernlike leaves which smell of aniseed and have a sugary taste. Clusters of small white flowers follow in summer. The leaves can be chopped into salads and omelettes or used to sweeten stewed fruit. Grow in moist soil.

6ft
5ft

OCIMUM BASILICUM ⓩ 9–10

BASIL

LAMIACEAE

A tender perennial usually treated as an annual with bright green leaves and white flowers. Buy and plant out after all danger of frost is over, or keep in a pot on the windowsill. There is an attractive purple-leaved form, 'Purpurascens', with pink flowers. Grow in fertile, well-drained soil. Cuttings root readily.

12–24in
12in

ORIGANUM VULGARE ⓩ 5–9

MARJORAM

LAMIACEAE

A perennial with soft evergreen leaves and violet flowers in midsummer. Easy to grow, marjoram is an attractive plant for the front of the flower border, in a pot, or in the herb garden. Look for the golden marjoram 'Aureum', which will brighten up the dullest of gardens. Grow in poor, well-drained soil.

12–36in
12–36in

≣ leaf type   light preference   ⚘ speed of growth   ✿ ease of growth

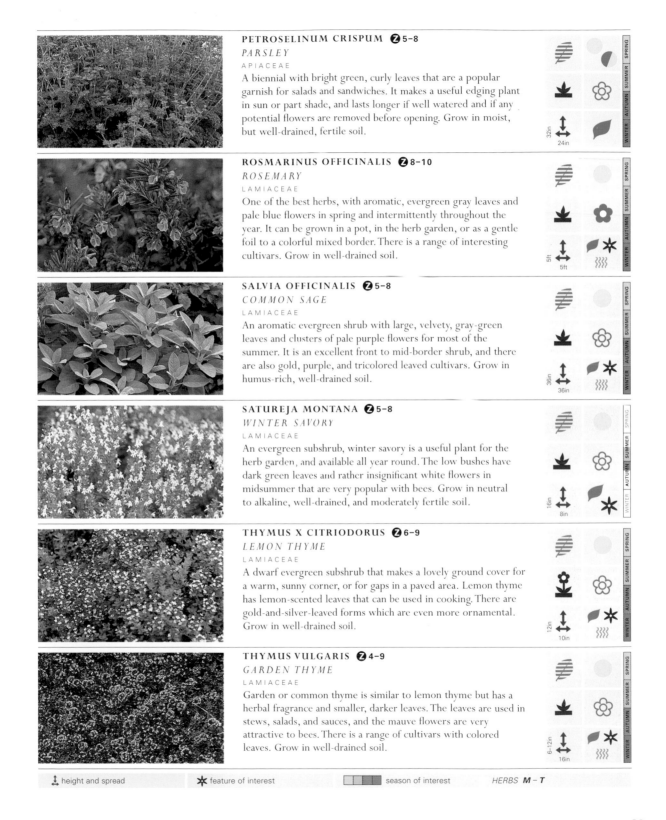

PETROSELINUM CRISPUM Ⓩ 5–8

PARSLEY

APIACEAE

A biennial with bright green, curly leaves that are a popular garnish for salads and sandwiches. It makes a useful edging plant in sun or part shade, and lasts longer if well watered and if any potential flowers are removed before opening. Grow in moist, but well-drained, fertile soil.

32in / 24in

ROSMARINUS OFFICINALIS Ⓩ 8–10

ROSEMARY

LAMIACEAE

One of the best herbs, with aromatic, evergreen gray leaves and pale blue flowers in spring and intermittently throughout the year. It can be grown in a pot, in the herb garden, or as a gentle foil to a colorful mixed border. There is a range of interesting cultivars. Grow in well-drained soil.

5ft / 5ft

SALVIA OFFICINALIS Ⓩ 5–8

COMMON SAGE

LAMIACEAE

An aromatic evergreen shrub with large, velvety, gray-green leaves and clusters of pale purple flowers for most of the summer. It is an excellent front to mid-border shrub, and there are also gold, purple, and tricolored leaved cultivars. Grow in humus-rich, well-drained soil.

36in / 36in

SATUREJA MONTANA Ⓩ 5–8

WINTER SAVORY

LAMIACEAE

An evergreen subshrub, winter savory is a useful plant for the herb garden, and available all year round. The low bushes have dark green leaves and rather insignificant white flowers in midsummer that are very popular with bees. Grow in neutral to alkaline, well-drained, and moderately fertile soil.

16in / 8in

THYMUS X CITRIODORUS Ⓩ 6–9

LEMON THYME

LAMIACEAE

A dwarf evergreen subshrub that makes a lovely ground cover for a warm, sunny corner, or for gaps in a paved area. Lemon thyme has lemon-scented leaves that can be used in cooking. There are gold-and-silver-leaved forms which are even more ornamental. Grow in well-drained soil.

12in / 10in

THYMUS VULGARIS Ⓩ 4–9

GARDEN THYME

LAMIACEAE

Garden or common thyme is similar to lemon thyme but has a herbal fragrance and smaller, darker leaves. The leaves are used in stews, salads, and sauces, and the mauve flowers are very attractive to bees. There is a range of cultivars with colored leaves. Grow in well-drained soil.

6–12in / 16in

↕ height and spread ✳ feature of interest ▭ season of interest *HERBS M – T*

PLANTS THAT CAN CAUSE SKIN RASHES

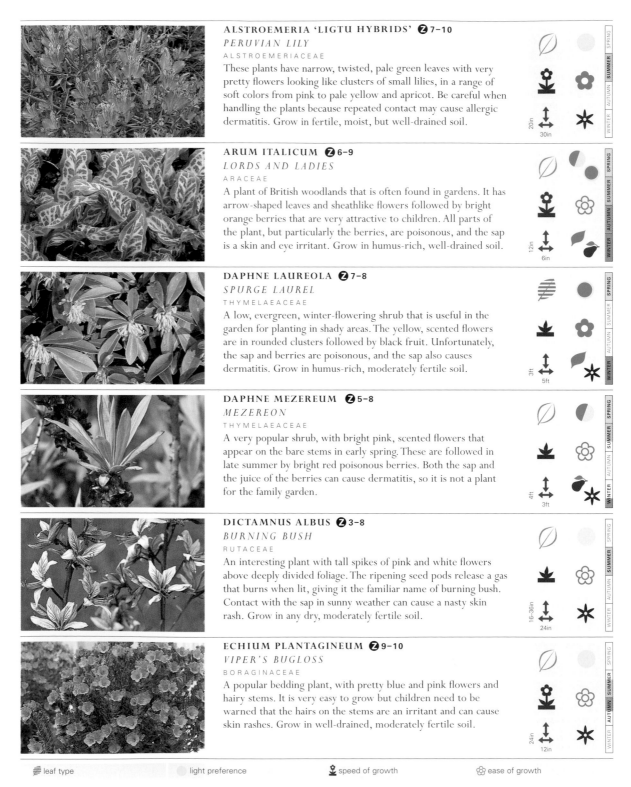

ALSTROEMERIA 'LIGTU HYBRIDS' ❷ 7–10
PERUVIAN LILY
ALSTROEMERIACEAE

These plants have narrow, twisted, pale green leaves with very pretty flowers looking like clusters of small lilies, in a range of soft colors from pink to pale yellow and apricot. Be careful when handling the plants because repeated contact may cause allergic dermatitis. Grow in fertile, moist, but well-drained soil.

ARUM ITALICUM ❷ 6–9
LORDS AND LADIES
ARACEAE

A plant of British woodlands that is often found in gardens. It has arrow-shaped leaves and sheathlike flowers followed by bright orange berries that are very attractive to children. All parts of the plant, but particularly the berries, are poisonous, and the sap is a skin and eye irritant. Grow in humus-rich, well-drained soil.

DAPHNE LAUREOLA ❷ 7–8
SPURGE LAUREL
THYMELAEACEAE

A low, evergreen, winter-flowering shrub that is useful in the garden for planting in shady areas. The yellow, scented flowers are in rounded clusters followed by black fruit. Unfortunately, the sap and berries are poisonous, and the sap also causes dermatitis. Grow in humus-rich, moderately fertile soil.

DAPHNE MEZEREUM ❷ 5–8
MEZEREON
THYMELAEACEAE

A very popular shrub, with bright pink, scented flowers that appear on the bare stems in early spring. These are followed in late summer by bright red poisonous berries. Both the sap and the juice of the berries can cause dermatitis, so it is not a plant for the family garden.

DICTAMNUS ALBUS ❷ 3–8
BURNING BUSH
RUTACEAE

An interesting plant with tall spikes of pink and white flowers above deeply divided foliage. The ripening seed pods release a gas that burns when lit, giving it the familiar name of burning bush. Contact with the sap in sunny weather can cause a nasty skin rash. Grow in any dry, moderately fertile soil.

ECHIUM PLANTAGINEUM ❷ 9–10
VIPER'S BUGLOSS
BORAGINACEAE

A popular bedding plant, with pretty blue and pink flowers and hairy stems. It is very easy to grow but children need to be warned that the hairs on the stems are an irritant and can cause skin rashes. Grow in well-drained, moderately fertile soil.

≣ leaf type   ● light preference   ♟ speed of growth   ✿ ease of growth

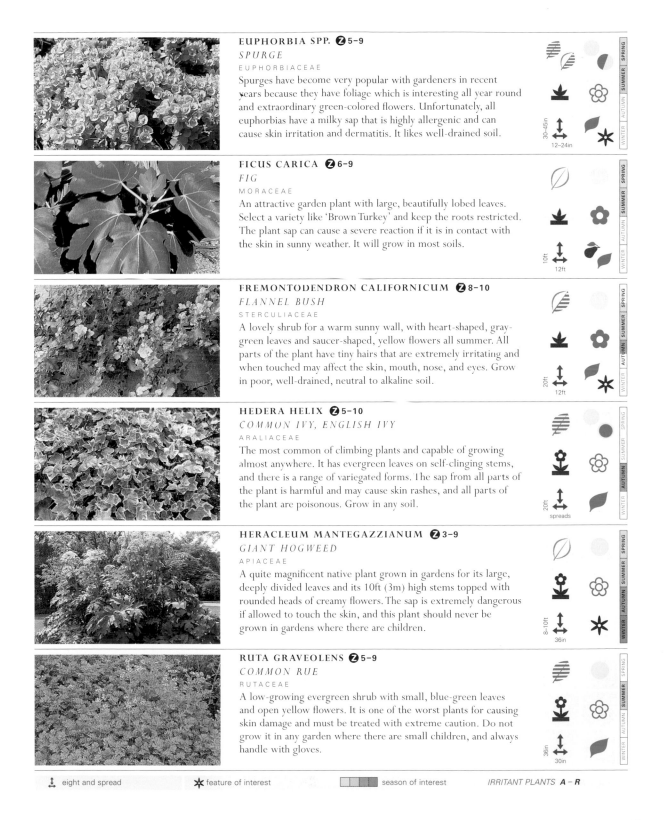

EUPHORBIA SPP. ❷ 5–9

SPURGE

EUPHORBIACEAE

Spurges have become very popular with gardeners in recent years because they have foliage which is interesting all year round and extraordinary green-colored flowers. Unfortunately, all euphorbias have a milky sap that is highly allergenic and can cause skin irritation and dermatitis. It likes well-drained soil.

30–45in
12–24in

FICUS CARICA ❷ 6–9

FIG

MORACEAE

An attractive garden plant with large, beautifully lobed leaves. Select a variety like 'Brown Turkey' and keep the roots restricted. The plant sap can cause a severe reaction if it is in contact with the skin in sunny weather. It will grow in most soils.

10ft
12ft

FREMONTODENDRON CALIFORNICUM ❷ 8–10

FLANNEL BUSH

STERCULIACEAE

A lovely shrub for a warm sunny wall, with heart-shaped, gray-green leaves and saucer-shaped, yellow flowers all summer. All parts of the plant have tiny hairs that are extremely irritating and when touched may affect the skin, mouth, nose, and eyes. Grow in poor, well-drained, neutral to alkaline soil.

20ft
12ft

HEDERA HELIX ❷ 5–10

COMMON IVY, ENGLISH IVY

ARALIACEAE

The most common of climbing plants and capable of growing almost anywhere. It has evergreen leaves on self-clinging stems, and there is a range of variegated forms. The sap from all parts of the plant is harmful and may cause skin rashes, and all parts of the plant are poisonous. Grow in any soil.

20ft
spreads

HERACLEUM MANTEGAZZIANUM ❷ 3–9

GIANT HOGWEED

APIACEAE

A quite magnificent native plant grown in gardens for its large, deeply divided leaves and its 10ft (3m) high stems topped with rounded heads of creamy flowers. The sap is extremely dangerous if allowed to touch the skin, and this plant should never be grown in gardens where there are children.

8–10ft
36in

RUTA GRAVEOLENS ❷ 5–9

COMMON RUE

RUTACEAE

A low-growing evergreen shrub with small, blue-green leaves and open yellow flowers. It is one of the worst plants for causing skin damage and must be treated with extreme caution. Do not grow it in any garden where there are small children, and always handle with gloves.

36in
30in

↕ eight and spread   ✻ feature of interest   ▭▭ season of interest   *IRRITANT PLANTS* **A – R**

PLANTS WITH THORNS AND PRICKLES

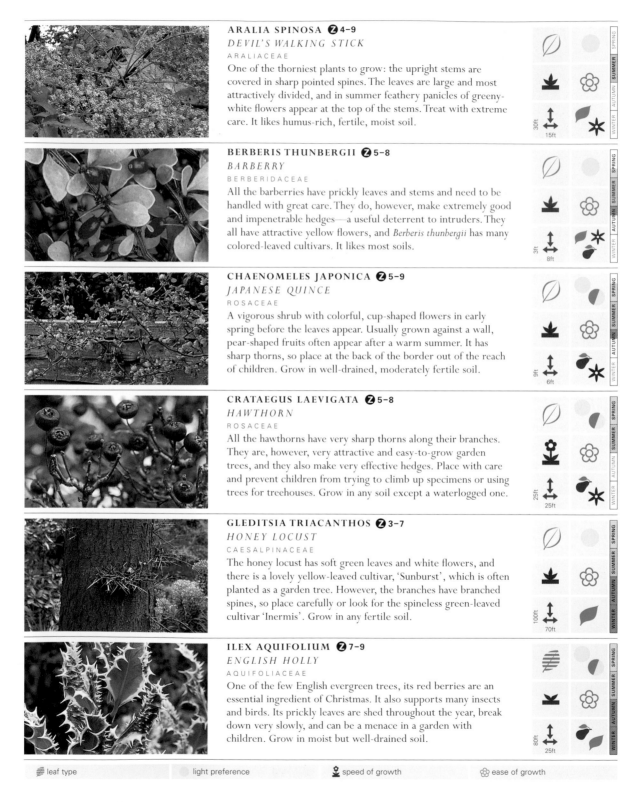

ARALIA SPINOSA ❷ 4–9
DEVIL'S WALKING STICK
ARALIACEAE

One of the thorniest plants to grow: the upright stems are covered in sharp pointed spines. The leaves are large and most attractively divided, and in summer feathery panicles of greeny-white flowers appear at the top of the stems. Treat with extreme care. It likes humus-rich, fertile, moist soil.

BERBERIS THUNBERGII ❷ 5–8
BARBERRY
BERBERIDACEAE

All the barberries have prickly leaves and stems and need to be handled with great care. They do, however, make extremely good and impenetrable hedges—a useful deterrent to intruders. They all have attractive yellow flowers, and *Berberis thunbergii* has many colored-leaved cultivars. It likes most soils.

CHAENOMELES JAPONICA ❷ 5–9
JAPANESE QUINCE
ROSACEAE

A vigorous shrub with colorful, cup-shaped flowers in early spring before the leaves appear. Usually grown against a wall, pear-shaped fruits often appear after a warm summer. It has sharp thorns, so place at the back of the border out of the reach of children. Grow in well-drained, moderately fertile soil.

CRATAEGUS LAEVIGATA ❷ 5–8
HAWTHORN
ROSACEAE

All the hawthorns have very sharp thorns along their branches. They are, however, very attractive and easy-to-grow garden trees, and they also make very effective hedges. Place with care and prevent children from trying to climb up specimens or using trees for treehouses. Grow in any soil except a waterlogged one.

GLEDITSIA TRIACANTHOS ❷ 3–7
HONEY LOCUST
CAESALPINACEAE

The honey locust has soft green leaves and white flowers, and there is a lovely yellow-leaved cultivar, 'Sunburst', which is often planted as a garden tree. However, the branches have branched spines, so place carefully or look for the spineless green-leaved cultivar 'Inermis'. Grow in any fertile soil.

ILEX AQUIFOLIUM ❷ 7–9
ENGLISH HOLLY
AQUIFOLIACEAE

One of the few English evergreen trees, its red berries are an essential ingredient of Christmas. It also supports many insects and birds. Its prickly leaves are shed throughout the year, break down very slowly, and can be a menace in a garden with children. Grow in moist but well-drained soil.

≣ leaf type   ● light preference   ⚓ speed of growth   ✿ ease of growth

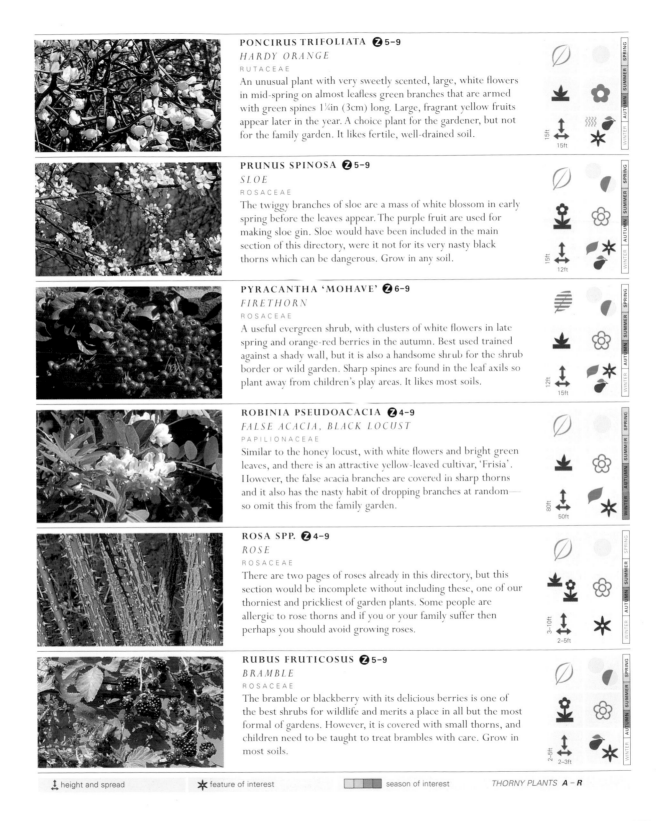

PONCIRUS TRIFOLIATA ⓩ5–9
HARDY ORANGE
RUTACEAE

An unusual plant with very sweetly scented, large, white flowers in mid-spring on almost leafless green branches that are armed with green spines 1¼in (3cm) long. Large, fragrant yellow fruits appear later in the year. A choice plant for the gardener, but not for the family garden. It likes fertile, well-drained soil.

15ft
15ft

PRUNUS SPINOSA ⓩ5–9
SLOE
ROSACEAE

The twiggy branches of sloe are a mass of white blossom in early spring before the leaves appear. The purple fruit are used for making sloe gin. Sloe would have been included in the main section of this directory, were it not for its very nasty black thorns which can be dangerous. Grow in any soil.

15ft
12ft

PYRACANTHA 'MOHAVE' ⓩ6–9
FIRETHORN
ROSACEAE

A useful evergreen shrub, with clusters of white flowers in late spring and orange-red berries in the autumn. Best used trained against a shady wall, but it is also a handsome shrub for the shrub border or wild garden. Sharp spines are found in the leaf axils so plant away from children's play areas. It likes most soils.

12ft
15ft

ROBINIA PSEUDOACACIA ⓩ4–9
FALSE ACACIA, BLACK LOCUST
PAPILIONACEAE

Similar to the honey locust, with white flowers and bright green leaves, and there is an attractive yellow-leaved cultivar, 'Frisia'. However, the false acacia branches are covered in sharp thorns and it also has the nasty habit of dropping branches at random—so omit this from the family garden.

80ft
50ft

ROSA SPP. ⓩ4–9
ROSE
ROSACEAE

There are two pages of roses already in this directory, but this section would be incomplete without including these, one of our thorniest and prickliest of garden plants. Some people are allergic to rose thorns and if you or your family suffer then perhaps you should avoid growing roses.

3–10ft
2–5ft

RUBUS FRUTICOSUS ⓩ5–9
BRAMBLE
ROSACEAE

The bramble or blackberry with its delicious berries is one of the best shrubs for wildlife and merits a place in all but the most formal of gardens. However, it is covered with small thorns, and children need to be taught to treat brambles with care. Grow in most soils.

2–5ft
2–3ft

⬍ height and spread   ✳ feature of interest   ▭▭▭ season of interest   *THORNY PLANTS* **A – R**

POISONOUS PLANTS

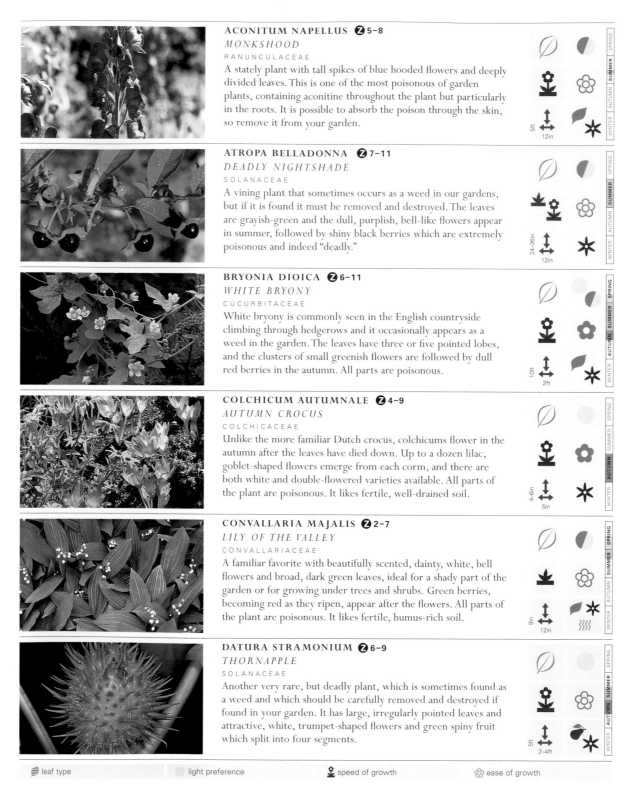

ACONITUM NAPELLUS **Z** 5–8
MONKSHOOD
RANUNCULACEAE

A stately plant with tall spikes of blue hooded flowers and deeply divided leaves. This is one of the most poisonous of garden plants, containing aconitine throughout the plant but particularly in the roots. It is possible to absorb the poison through the skin, so remove it from your garden.

5ft / 12in

ATROPA BELLADONNA **Z** 7–11
DEADLY NIGHTSHADE
SOLANACEAE

A vining plant that sometimes occurs as a weed in our gardens, but if it is found it must be removed and destroyed. The leaves are grayish-green and the dull, purplish, bell-like flowers appear in summer, followed by shiny black berries which are extremely poisonous and indeed "deadly."

24–36in / 12in

BRYONIA DIOICA **Z** 6–11
WHITE BRYONY
CUCURBITACEAE

White bryony is commonly seen in the English countryside climbing through hedgerows and it occasionally appears as a weed in the garden. The leaves have three or five pointed lobes, and the clusters of small greenish flowers are followed by dull red berries in the autumn. All parts are poisonous.

10ft / 2ft

COLCHICUM AUTUMNALE **Z** 4–9
AUTUMN CROCUS
COLCHICACEAE

Unlike the more familiar Dutch crocus, colchicums flower in the autumn after the leaves have died down. Up to a dozen lilac, goblet-shaped flowers emerge from each corm, and there are both white and double-flowered varieties available. All parts of the plant are poisonous. It likes fertile, well-drained soil.

4–6in / 5in

CONVALLARIA MAJALIS **Z** 2–7
LILY OF THE VALLEY
CONVALLARIACEAE

A familiar favorite with beautifully scented, dainty, white, bell flowers and broad, dark green leaves, ideal for a shady part of the garden or for growing under trees and shrubs. Green berries, becoming red as they ripen, appear after the flowers. All parts of the plant are poisonous. It likes fertile, humus-rich soil.

9in / 12in

DATURA STRAMONIUM **Z** 6–9
THORNAPPLE
SOLANACEAE

Another very rare, but deadly plant, which is sometimes found as a weed and which should be carefully removed and destroyed if found in your garden. It has large, irregularly pointed leaves and attractive, white, trumpet-shaped flowers and green spiny fruit which split into four segments.

5ft / 2–4ft

≣ leaf type   ● light preference   ♨ speed of growth   ✿ ease of growth

DIGITALIS PURPUREA ❷ 4–8
FOXGLOVE
SCROPHULARIACEAE

A common plant of the English woodland but now frequently grown in the garden, the foxglove has large hairy leaves and tall spikes of hanging purple or white tubular flowers and green fruits. All parts of the plant are poisonous, so remove all plants to avoid children playing with the flowers.

3–6ft
24in

EUONYMUS EUROPAEUS ❷ 4–7
SPINDLE
CELASTRACEAE

There are various species of euonymus grown in the garden, some with deciduous leaves turning red in autumn. The flowers are insignificant but are followed by pink fleshy fruit that split open to reveal bright orange seeds. All parts of the plant are poisonous.

10ft
8ft

HYOSCYAMUS NIGER ❷ 10–11
HENBANE
SOLANACEAE

Another rare, but dangerous, native plant that is occasionally found as a garden weed. A very distinctive plant, it is covered in sticky hairs with thick stems, lobed leaves, yellowish funnel-shaped flowers and green fruits. All parts are extremely poisonous—remove on sight in the garden.

24–36in
36in

IPOMOEA TRICOLOR ❷ 2–11
MORNING GLORY
CONVOLVULACEAE

Grown as an annual climber for its clear blue, trumpet flowers, which appear in the morning and fade in the afternoon, but are replaced by more flowers that open the next day. Quite easy to grow from seed, but the seeds themselves contain a halucinogenic substance and are dangerous if eaten. It likes most soils.

10–12ft
13ft

LABURNUM ANAGYROIDES ❷ 6–8
GOLDEN RAIN TREE
PAPILIONACEAE

A small tree with hanging bunches of yellow flowers in spring, followed by green pods containing black, shiny, extremely poisonous seeds that are very attractive to children. A few seeds can prove fatal, so never grow laburnums where there are young children. It will grow in most soils.

25ft
25ft

LANTANA CAMARA ❷ 10–11
YELLOW SAGE
VERBENACEACE

This is usually grown as a conservatory plant brought out into the garden for the summer. A shrub with coarse, pointed leaves and round clusters of yellow, orange, pink, or red flowers, the leaves, flowers, and particularly the unripe fruit are poisonous. Avoid growing it in the family garden.

3–6ft
3–6ft

⇕ height and spread   ✳ feature of interest   season of interest   *POISONOUS PLANTS* **A – L**

POISONOUS PLANTS

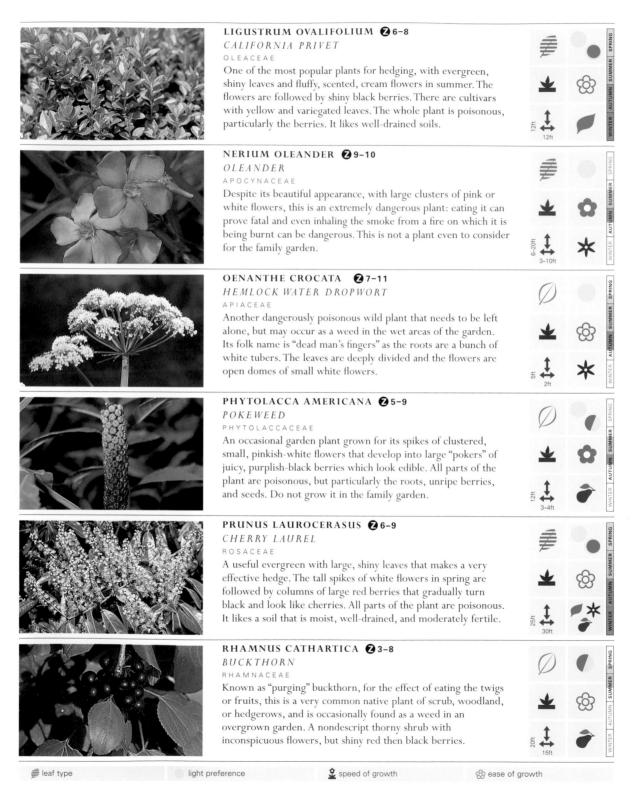

LIGUSTRUM OVALIFOLIUM ❷6–8

CALIFORNIA PRIVET

OLEACEAE

One of the most popular plants for hedging, with evergreen, shiny leaves and fluffy, scented, cream flowers in summer. The flowers are followed by shiny black berries. There are cultivars with yellow and variegated leaves. The whole plant is poisonous, particularly the berries. It likes well-drained soils.

12ft / 12ft

NERIUM OLEANDER ❷9–10

OLEANDER

APOCYNACEAE

Despite its beautiful appearance, with large clusters of pink or white flowers, this is an extremely dangerous plant: eating it can prove fatal and even inhaling the smoke from a fire on which it is being burnt can be dangerous. This is not a plant even to consider for the family garden.

6–20ft / 3–10ft

OENANTHE CROCATA ❷7–11

HEMLOCK WATER DROPWORT

APIACEAE

Another dangerously poisonous wild plant that needs to be left alone, but may occur as a weed in the wet areas of the garden. Its folk name is "dead man's fingers" as the roots are a bunch of white tubers. The leaves are deeply divided and the flowers are open domes of small white flowers.

5ft / 2ft

PHYTOLACCA AMERICANA ❷5–9

POKEWEED

PHYTOLACCACEAE

An occasional garden plant grown for its spikes of clustered, small, pinkish-white flowers that develop into large "pokers" of juicy, purplish-black berries which look edible. All parts of the plant are poisonous, but particularly the roots, unripe berries, and seeds. Do not grow it in the family garden.

12ft / 3–4ft

PRUNUS LAUROCERASUS ❷6–9

CHERRY LAUREL

ROSACEAE

A useful evergreen with large, shiny leaves that makes a very effective hedge. The tall spikes of white flowers in spring are followed by columns of large red berries that gradually turn black and look like cherries. All parts of the plant are poisonous. It likes a soil that is moist, well-drained, and moderately fertile.

25ft / 30ft

RHAMNUS CATHARTICA ❷3–8

BUCKTHORN

RHAMNACEAE

Known as "purging" buckthorn, for the effect of eating the twigs or fruits, this is a very common native plant of scrub, woodland, or hedgerows, and is occasionally found as a weed in an overgrown garden. A nondescript thorny shrub with inconspicuous flowers, but shiny red then black berries.

20ft / 15ft

≡ leaf type   ○ light preference   ♨ speed of growth   ✿ ease of growth

RICINUS COMMUNIS ❷ 9–10
CASTOR-OIL PLANT
EUPHORBIACEAE

A very dramatic plant, with shiny red leaves frequently seen in summer bedding plantings. This is perhaps the most dangerous plant grown in our gardens, as handling the plant can cause sore skin and the whole plant, but particularly the seeds, contains a deadly poison. Never grow it in your family garden.

6–10ft / 36in

SOLANUM DULCAMARA ❷ 4–10
WOODY NIGHTSHADE
SOLANACEAE

A vining plant that can be found scrambling through hedgerows and small trees, but it is also planted in the garden for its attractive purple flowers, each with a central yellow cone. The bunches of small round fruits are green, and then red when ripe. The unripe fruits are particularly poisonous.

3–6ft / 6–8in

SOLANUM NIGRUM ❷ 6–9
BLACK NIGHTSHADE
SOLANACEAE

This annual is a common weed of wasteland and gardens. The clusters of white, potatolike flowers are followed by bunches of shiny black berries. All parts of the plant are extremely poisonous, but particularly the unripe berries, so remove any plants you find in the garden and destroy them.

20in / 12in

TAMUS COMMUNIS ❷ 7–11
BLACK BRYONY
DIOSCOREACEAE

A twining plant with glossy, heart-shaped leaves and clusters of greenish-yellow flowers, its fruit are round, shiny green berries that turn black when ripe. The sap is a severe irritant and all parts of the plant are poisonous.

10ft / 1–2ft

TAXUS BACCATA ❷ 7–8
YEW
TAXACEAE

One of the best conifers for clipped hedges and the backbone of the formal garden, yew is almost indispensable with its shiny, dark green needles all year round and its bright red "berries". Unfortunately, the leaves and seeds are poisonous. It likes well-drained, fertile soil.

30–70ft / 25–30ft

VERATRUM NIGRUM ❷ 6–9
BLACK HELLEBORE
MELANTHIACEAE

A choice statuesque plant for the shady garden, with very large ribbed leaves and tall flower spikes of closely packed, dark red flowers. The small seed pods turn black as they ripen. All parts of the plant, but particularly the roots and leaves, are toxic. This is definitely not a plant to include in the family garden.

36–48in / 24in

⇳ height and spread   ✳ feature of interest   ▮▮▮▮ season of interest   *POISONOUS PLANTS L – V*

GLOSSARY

ALPINE: A plant that in its natural mountain habitat grows above the uppermost limit of trees. More colloquially, plants that are suitable for rock gardens are called alpines.

ANNUAL: A plant that grows from seed, flowers, and dies within the same year. Some half-hardy perennial plants are used as annuals; that is, they die off in the winter.

AQUATIC PLANT: A plant that lives totally or partly submerged in water.

AXIL: The upper angle between leaf and stem.

BEDDING PLANTS: Plants that are set out for a temporary spring or summer display and discarded at the end of the season.

BIENNIAL: A plant raised from seed that makes its initial growth in one year and flowers during the following one, then dies.

BOG GARDEN PLANTS: Plants that live with their roots in moist soil.

BULB: An underground food storage organ formed of fleshy, modified leaves that enclose a dormant shoot.

CALYX: The outer and protective part of a flower. It is usually green and is very apparent in roses.

COMPOST: Vegetable waste from kitchens, as well as the soft parts of garden plants, which is encouraged to decompose and to form a material that can be dug into soil or used to create a mulch around plants.

CORM: An underground storage organ formed of a swollen stem base; for example, a gladiolus.

CULTIVAR: A shortened term for "cultivated variety" that indicates a variety raised in cultivation. Strictly speaking, most modern varieties are cultivars, but the term variety is still widely used because it is familiar to most gardeners.

CUTTING: A section of plant which is detached and encouraged to form roots and stems to provide a new independent plant. Cuttings may be taken from roots, stems, or leaves.

DEADHEADING: The removal of a faded flower head to prevent the formation of seeds and to encourage the development of further flowers.

DORMANT: When a plant is alive but is making no growth, it is called dormant. The dormant period is usually the winter.

EVERGREEN: Plants that appear to be green throughout the year and not to lose their leaves are called evergreen. In reality, however, they shed some of their leaves throughout the year, while producing others.

FRIABLE: Soil that is crumbly light, and easily worked. It especially applies to soil being prepared as a seedbed in spring.

HALF-HARDY: A plant that can withstand fairly low temperatures, but needs protection from frost.

HALF-HARDY ANNUAL: An annual that is sown in gentle warmth in a greenhouse in spring, the seedlings being transferred to wider spacings in pots or boxes. The plants are placed in a garden or container only when all risk of frost has passed.

HARDEN OFF: To accustom plants raised under cover to cooler conditions so they can be planted outside.

HARDY: A plant that is able to survive outdoors in winter. In the case of some rock-garden plants, good drainage is essential to ensure their survival. Also refers to a plant that can withstand extremes of growth conditions.

HERB: A plant that is grown for its aromatic qualities and can often be used in cooking or medicinally.

HERBACEOUS PERENNIAL: A plant with no woody tissue that lives for several years. Herbaceous perennials may be deciduous or evergreen.

HYBRID: A cross between two different species, varieties, or genera.

LOAM: Friable topsoil.

MARGINAL PLANTS: Plants that live in shallow water at the edges of ponds. Some also thrive in boggy soil surrounding a pond.

MULCHING: Covering the soil around plants with well-decayed organic material, such as garden compost, peat, or, in the case of rock-garden plants, stone chippings or ¼ in (6mm) gravel.

NEUTRAL: Soil that is neither acid nor alkaline, with a pH of 7.0, is said to be neutral. Most plants grow in a pH of about 6.5.

PEAT: A naturally occurring substance formed from partly rotted organic material in water-logged soils, used as a growing medium and soil additive.

PERENNIAL: Any plant that lives for three or more years is called a perennial.

PERGOLA: An open timber structure made up of linked arches.

POTTING SOIL: Traditionally, a soil formed of loam, sharp sand and peat, fertilizers, and lime. The ratio of the ingredients is altered according to whether the soil is used for sowing seeds, potting-up, or repotting plants into larger containers. Recognition of the environmental importance of conserving peat beds has led to many modern soils being formed of other organic materials, such as coir or shredded bark.

PRICKING OFF: Transplanting seedlings from the container in which they were sown to one where they are more widely spaced.

RACEME: An elongated flower head with each flower having a stem.

RAISED BED: A raised area, usually encircled by a drystone wall. Rock garden plants can be grown both in the raised bed and the wall.

RHIZOME: An underground or partly buried horizontal stem. It can be slender or fleshy. Some irises have thick, fleshy rhizomes, while those of lily-of-the-valley are slender and creeping. They act as storage organs and perpetuate plants from one season to another.

SCREE BED: An area formed of small stones, together with a few large rocks, often positioned at the base of a rock garden.

SEED LEAVES: The first leaves that develop on a seedling, which are coarser and more robust than the true leaves.

SEMIEVERGREEN: A plant that may keep some of its leaves in a reason-ably mild winter.

SPECIES ROSE: A term for a wild rose or one of its near relatives.

STAMEN: The male part of a flower.

STANDARD: A tree or shrub trained to form a rounded head of branches at the top of a clear stem.

SUBSHRUB: Small and spreading shrub with a woody base. It differs from normal shrubs in that, when

grown in temperate regions, its upper stems and shoots die back during winter.

TENDER: A plant that will not tolerate cold conditions.

TOPSOIL: The uppermost fertile layer of soil that is suitable for plant growth.

TROUGH GARDENS: Old stone troughs partly filled with drainage material and then with freely draining soil. They are planted with miniature conifers and bulbs, as well as small rock-garden plants. These features are usually displayed on terraces and patios.

TUBER: A swollen, thickened, and fleshy stem or root. Some tubers are swollen roots (dahlia), while others are swollen stems (potato). They serve as storage organs and help to perpetuate plants from one season to another.

VARIEGATED: Usually applied to leaves and used to describe a state of having two or more colours.

VARIETY: A naturally occurring variation of a species that retains its characteristics when propagated. The term is often used for cultivars.

WILDLIFE POND: An informal pond, often positioned toward the far end of a garden, which encourages the presence of wildlife such as frogs, birds, insects, and small mammals.

INDEX

HARDINESS ZONES MAP

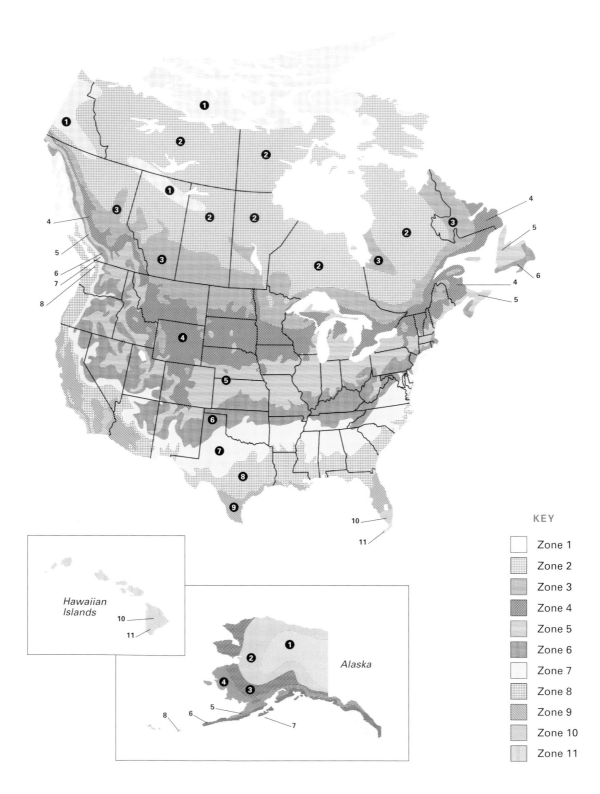

Hawaiian
Islands

10
11

Alaska

8
6   5
7

KEY

Zone 1
Zone 2
Zone 3
Zone 4
Zone 5
Zone 6
Zone 7
Zone 8
Zone 9
Zone 10
Zone 11